The Word Whiz's

Greatest Hits

Middle School Edition

By Chris Kensler

A Paper Airplane Project

Simon & Schuster

New York ● London ● Sydney ● Singapore ● Toronto

Kaplan Publishing
Published by Simon & Schuster, Inc.
1230 Avenue of the Americas
New York, NY 10020

For bulk sales to schools, colleges, and universities, please contact: Order Department, Simon & Schuster, 100 Front Street, Riverside, NJ 08075. Phone: 1-800-223-2336. Fax: 1-800-943-9831.

Kaplan® is a registered trademark of Kaplan, Inc.

Cover Design: Cheung Tai
Interior Page Design and Production: Heather Kern

Manufactured in the United States of America

January 2002

10 9 8 7 6 5 4 3 2 1

Library of Congress Cataloging-in-Publication Data

ISBN 0-7432-1109-X

All of the practice questions in this book were created by the authors to illustrate question types. They are not actual test questions.

Table of Contents

About the Author

Chris Kensler grew up in Indiana and attended Indiana University, where he majored in English. He has worked as an educational book editor, covered the presidential campaign for a major news organization, run a national digital arts and culture magazine, and written several titles for kids, including *Study Smart Junior*, which received the Parents' Choice Award.

Grady Goode is a figment of his imagination.

Acknowledgments

The author would like to thank Maureen McMahon and Lori DeGeorge for their help in shaping and editing the manuscript.

The publisher wishes to thank Margaret Rodero and Ryan Blanchette for their contributions to this book.

Dedication

For Louise Sebene

Introduction

Hi. My name is Grady. Grady Goode. As you
can probably guess from the name they gave me, my parents have been very interested in my academic success from Day One. Right after I learned to say "Mommy" and "Daddy," I was taught the phrase "Grady Goode gets good grades." Seriously, I could say it when I was eleven months old. My parents have a tape recording of it. My parents are strange people.

Anyway, now I'm in the eighth grade. At my school I'm famous for three things—an encyclopedic knowledge of sports statistics, a freakish grasp of celebrity trivia, and a truly massive vocabulary. I have read books, magazine stories, and newspaper articles about ball players from Babe Ruth to John Elway. And when it comes to movie stars and pop singers, go ahead and ask me anything about Britney Spears or David Spade or Penelope Cruz or anyone else famous. By reading everything there is to read on my favorite subjects, and by just generally paying attention to words, I have become my school's Word Whiz. Now I'm going to turn you into one.

If you're having trouble on tests, one reason might be because you are having trouble understanding the words used on them. Of course, the first and most likely reason you blank or panic or freak out on tests is that instead of studying, you keep watching your new *Chicken Run* DVD. (Believe me, I don't hold it against you, that flick rocks.) Still, sometimes things don't go so well even when you do study. That's the worst. You're like—I studied all night and I still got a D! What's up with that?

Sometimes it's because you just aren't comfortable with the words on the test. For example, say you are taking a math test and one of the questions asks you to find the "perimeter of a rectangle." It's not hard to do—you just add up all the sides. But if you space out on what the word "perimeter" means, you're in trouble. Your brain freezes. Does it have something to do with periscopes? Or maybe something to do with meters? The next thing you know, you have a picture of a submarine doing the 40-meter dash in your head.

I've been there. It's no fun. But it doesn't have to be that way.

Word Whiz Is Here to Help

Believe it or not, you probably already know more than 10,000 words total. It just happens. The older you get, the more words get added to your vocabulary. But let's not talk about the words you already know, let's focus on the words you need to know. The 600-plus words in this book are the most important ones to know for middle school homework, exams, and standardized tests. I call them WhizWords. If you know these WhizWords backward and forward, you will be in good shape at school, and you will no doubt become rich and successful when you grow up.

I'm going to review these WhizWords for you by relating them to things

you're probably interested in, like TV, movies, sports, music, celebrities, and the stuff kids like us like to do when we're NOT in school. All these things can help you learn the 600-plus words in this book.

I'm also going to explain them to you in words you already know. The problem with a lot of dictionaries is the words they use in the definition are harder than the word they are defining! Or they just repeat the word. Here's an example—the definition of "impartial" from a popular dictionary (I won't name names):

impartial—*adj.* not partial; unprejudiced.

Gee, thanks. If I knew what "partial" meant, I could probably figure out impartial. And "unprejudiced?" How many syllables is that? Eleven? Geez. And of course they don't give a sample sentence. Now here's my definition:

impartial—*adj.* fair. Judges and juries are supposed to be <u>impartial</u>. That means they just go by the facts. Like Judge Judy on TV —she is an <u>impartial</u> judge who listens to all the facts, then she reams the person who is guilty.

Better, right? I'm also only going to give you the one or two meanings that you are most likely to see on a test or in class. Some words have tons of different meanings, and regular dictionaries have to list them all. But in my book, I am just going to focus on the meanings that apply to your tests, classroom reading, and homework.

How to Use This Book

Most dictionaries just list all words in alphabetical order. It makes perfect sense. But I have gone one step further. My WhizWords are divided into six categories:

English Language Arts　　**Test Instructions**
Social Studies　　　　　　**Science**
Math　　　　　　　　　　**All-Purpose Words**

This way, you can focus on the subjects where you want to improve your vocabulary. I've also included a list of words that often appear in the instructions on tests, and another list of "all-purpose" words.

Each of these chapters has two parts—1) the vocabulary list, and 2) some practice exercises. The exercises will help you remember important words that are related to each other. Off to the side of the exercises, you'll see a bunch of icons. These tell you what resources you'll use for the exercise— things like TV, newspapers, and the Internet. These are the icons:

Life　　School　　Movie　　Sports　　Magazine

History　Imagination　News　　Internet　Television

Think of these exercises as dessert. The main course of the book is my WhizWord lists. They give you easy-to-understand definitions and sample sentences like the one I gave you for "impartial." You'll also find all this extra cool stuff:

Whiz Tip My helpful hints on how to learn words and ace tests.

Whiz Quiz *Really* short quizzes to help cement the words in your brain.

Whiz Fact Good stuff to know that is related to a WhizWord.

DOUBLE MEANING WhizWords that mean different things in different subjects.

Synonym Words that mean the same thing as a WhizWord.

Antonym Words that mean the opposite of a WhizWord.

Related Word An important word related to a WhizWord.

On the Test How WhizWords are likely to appear on lots of tests.

Okay then. I think I'm done explaining. Have fun, and remember, if you learn all these words, your vocabulary will be really, really good and you should do better on your tests. It's a better way to live. Peace.

Grady Goode

Chapter 1
English Language Arts

Use an adjective or adverb to describe each of these words:
school
shopping
tests
green
sports
chewy

adjective—*n*. a word that describes a noun or a pronoun. You need to be able to pick out <u>adjectives</u> in sentences, and you also need to use them for your own writing. *Bad, good, smart, rich,* and *poor* are all <u>adjectives</u>.

adverb—*n*. a word that describes a verb, an adjective, or another adverb. What I just said for adjectives goes for <u>adverbs</u>. You can remember which words an <u>adverb</u> modifies because the parts of speech it modifies are part of its name: <u>ad</u>- (adjectives, adverbs) and -<u>verb</u> (verbs). *Very, really, not, incredibly, amazingly* and *obviously* are all <u>adverbs</u>.

alliteration—*n*. the use of two or more words with the same initial sound in a sentence or phrase. *Example*: *S*lothy *S.* *S*lothster *s*ank *s*lowly into the *s*ofa, *s*ighing.

almanac—*n*. an annual reference book that gives various facts and figures in tabular form. You can use an <u>almanac</u> to find average temperatures, elected officials, and all of the World Series winners.

analogy—*n*. a comparison between two things, made in order to explain or clarify an idea. *Example*: Pop music fans and hard rock fans can't stand each other's music. *Oil and water do not mix.*

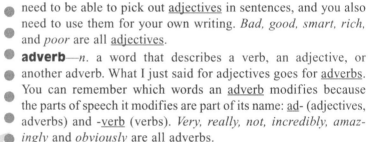

Use an analogy to a staircase to describe how your grades have been going recently:

_____
_____
_____

analyze—*v*. to study carefully to figure out something. I must say, after <u>analyzing</u> all the latest Internet search engines, I still like Yahoo! the best. It is fast, gets me the best results, and is easiest to navigate.

antonym—*n*. a word that means the opposite. *Good* is the <u>antonym</u> of *bad*. *Over* is the <u>antonym</u> of *under*. I have listed <u>antonyms</u> for lots of words throughout this book.

analysis—**n.**
close study.

article—*n*. a word that signals a noun. *Example*: *A, an,* and *the* are examples of <u>articles</u>.

assonance—*n*. a partial rhyme where the vowels rhyme, but the consonants do not. *Example*: The ball was hit at Carl, but he was looking at the stars, so it hit him in the arm.

atlas—*n*. a book of maps. You can use an <u>atlas</u> to find geographical information.

bibliography—*n*. the list of sources used as research in a book or paper. *Example*: The <u>bibliography</u> for my research paper on baked beans included the book *Hormel: Can of Plenty*, by G.A.S. Flame, published in 1923 by Bacon Books.

character development—*n*. the building of a character in a story, piece by piece. The pieces used to build a character include physical descriptions, behavior, relationships with other characters, and reactions to occurrences.

characteristic—*n*. special quality. In English language arts, physical <u>characteristics</u> are often used to describe a character in a story or the story's setting. *Example:* Some <u>characteristics</u> of Frankenstein include a high, square forehead and rivets coming out of the sides of his head.

clarify—*v*. to make clearer. On tests, you will often be asked to <u>clarify</u> sentences and what characters in stories are talking about. *Example*: "Jim Carrey's comedic brilliance over the span of his film career is unsurpassed in the history of cinema" can be <u>clarified</u> as "Jim Carrey is funnier than anyone, ever."

clause—*n*. a group of words that contains a subject and a predicate.

cliché—*n*. a saying that is used too much. *Example*: It is a <u>cliché</u> to call cafeteria food dog food, because so many people have called it dog food before. In general, when writing a story, you want to avoid using <u>clichés</u>.

climax—*n*. the big event that a story builds toward. Stories of suspense usually have the biggest, best <u>climaxes</u> because the whole point of a suspense story is to get you on the edge of your seat and then have a big bang at the end.

compare—*v*. to find the similarities. (See *contrast* for more.)

complex—*adj*. complicated, made up of a bunch of connected parts. On lots of tests you are asked to read <u>complex</u> passages and find the important information in them. It's like watching a murder mystery on TV and trying to figure out who did it. The mystery is <u>complex</u>, but if you pay attention and concentrate, you can figure out who the culprit is.

compound sentence—*n*. a sentence made up of two complete

WhizTip

To remember characteristics, **think of the word "character"**—characters have characteristics.

Antonym

simple—**adj.** easy.

9

sentences, usually joined with a conjunction or a conjunction and a comma. *Example*: I really like her, but I am afraid to talk to her.

compound word—*n.* a word made of two or more other words. *Carpetbagger* (carpet + bagger) is a compound word. (See Social Studies for the definition of *carpetbagger*.)

conclusion—*n.* judgment or decision. Many tests ask you what conclusion you can draw from a passage or what conclusion someone in a story came to. That just means you need to be able to sum up what you read. *Example*: After I read the Cleveland Indians' team stats, I came to the conclusion that they need a few more good pitchers. Only three pitchers on the team had winning records!

conflict—*n.* a clash of ideas; a clash of characters. Most interesting stories center around conflict—two people who can't stand each other, or two ideas that are really different. *Example*: I am writing a screenplay called *Pretty Dumb* about two actresses who can't stand each other. There is a lot of conflict between the two.

conjunction—*n.* a word that joins words or groups of words in a sentence. There are only a handful of them. The most common are: *and, or, for, but, yet.*

consistent—*adj.* in agreement; compatible. On English language arts tests, your answers should be consistent with the information in the reading passages.

context—*n.* the setting a word or statement appears in. It's important to know context when you are trying to figure out what someone means. If someone yells "Stop!" the context of that yell tells you why she is yelling. Is her car being stolen? Or is someone about to drive off a cliff? If you know the context, you'll understand what is meant.

contrast—*v.* to find the differences. This word is most often used in test questions that ask you to "compare and contrast." That just means you should write about the similarities and the differences. *Example*: Compare and contrast supermodel/actress James King and actress/pin-up star Pamela Anderson.

credible—*adj.* believable. In a trial, a credible witness is a witness the jury can believe. On a test, a credible answer is one that you think could be true. So if I said Pamela Anderson and James King are the best actresses in the world, that's not really a credible statement. If I said both are blonde and beautiful—that's credible.

dialect—*n.* the manner in which a particular part of a country speaks. Where you come from is usually where you get your dialect: there is a soft Southern dialect; the twangy Texas dialect; the hard-edged New England dialect. Authors use dialect in stories to give readers information about character and setting.

dialogue—*n.* the spoken conversations written in a book or a play, usually in quotation marks. Here's some dialogue from

Pretty Dumb, the screenplay I'm writing for supermodel James King and actress Pamela Anderson. "Hey Pam—my blonde hair is a mess. Poor me. What brand of conditioner do you use?" asked James. "I use Fanteen Selectives with blonde highlights," Pamela replied. "But you can't borrow it."

dictionary—*n.* a reference book containing all sorts of information about words, including their definitions, pronunciation, parts of speech, origins, roots, and usage.

edit—*v.* to revise or change a piece of writing to make it better. A good way to <u>edit</u> your own writing is to read it like someone else wrote it. Pick someone who you don't like; that way you'll be extra tough on the writing. (I usually pretend Christina Aguilera wrote whatever I'm <u>editing</u>. I don't know why, she just rubs me the wrong way.)

euphemism—*n.* the act of substituting an inoffensive word or phrase for an offensive one. For example, "passed away" is a <u>euphemism</u> for "died." "We are in a rebuilding year" is a <u>euphemism</u> in sports for "We are terrible this year, please be patient."

evaluate—*v.* to consider. Tests ask you to <u>evaluate</u> information all of the time. That just means you need to read everything they give you and consider the information before making a decision on an answer. My dad often <u>evaluates</u> the food at the grocery store by looking at the ingredients to see how much fat is in it. He hates fat.

exposition—*n.* a detailed description or explanation of a subject. If you are asked to write an <u>expository</u> essay, your teacher wants you to explain or describe a subject in detail. That's <u>exposition</u>.

figurative language—*n.* the use of similes and metaphors. Instead of writing "Peyton Manning has a strong arm," a sports reporter using <u>figurative language</u> would write, "Peyton Manning's arm is like a cannon." (See the definitions for *simile* and *metaphor* for more on this.)

flashback—*n.* a point in a story where the narrative goes back in time for a little while before continuing forward. Books and movies use <u>flashbacks</u> all the time, usually to give you more information about a character or the plot. Sometimes in movies and on TV, they signal a <u>flashback</u> by making the screen get all wiggly or fuzzy.

foreshadow—*v.* to hint at what is to come later in a story. A writer may <u>foreshadow</u> that two young characters are going to get married later in the book by having each of them, separately, talk to people about how much they want to get married when they get older.

formal—*adj.* done in a proper way. Think of a <u>formal</u> statement or letter as a statement or letter dressed in a tuxedo. It is stiff, rigid, proper, and perfect. A <u>formal</u> essay is well organized and

List three euphemisms you or members of your family use:

1. _____
   _____
2. _____
   _____
3. _____
   _____
   _____

Remember flashback by thinking of the word "back."

Remember foreshadow by thinking of the word "forward."

English Language Arts

- follows all the rules of grammar and punctuation.

- **genre**—*n.* a type of writing. Romance, horror, mystery, and sci-fi are all fiction <u>genres</u>. My favorite <u>genre</u> is horror, especially R. L. Stine horror.

- **hyperbole**—*n.* an exaggeration used as a figure of speech. *Example:* The Green Bay Packers haven't won the Super Bowl in a million years.

- **identify**—*v.* to pick out. English language arts tests often ask you to <u>identify</u> the protagonist or to <u>identify</u> the verb or to <u>identify</u> the simile.

- **idiom**—*n.* a word or phrase that means something it doesn't really mean. Confused? Here are a few <u>idioms</u>:
  - *ants in your pants* means *you are fidgety*
  - *born with a silver spoon in your mouth* means *your parents are rich*
  - *stop bugging me* means *stop bothering me*

- **imagery**—*n.* mental pictures; the use of figurative language to create scenes and moods. Writers use <u>imagery</u> to make their stories more interesting. Here's an example from my screenplay, with the <u>imagery</u> underlined: Pamela Anderson rose from bed and <u>stretched like a baby penguin breaking from its egg</u>. She had a hard day ahead. She and James King were up for the same part in the new Jim Carrey movie. Whoever got the part would be the toast of the town. Whoever lost would feel <u>lower than the dirt on the soles of a pair of six-inch stiletto heels</u>. The movie's director, Fabio, held their fates in his hands.

- **index**—*n.* an alphabetized listing of names and places in a book, along with the pages they're mentioned on (usually found at the back of a book).

- **interjection**—*n.* an exclamation that stands alone. *Examples:* Holy cow! Mercy! Yo!

- **internal rhyme**—*n.* rhyme between a word within a line and at the end of the line, or between two words within two different lines. *Example:* A talking fly in my gravy said "Hi."

- **interview**—*n.* a conversation in which one person asks the questions and the other answers. One great way to learn about lots of different people is to read <u>interviews</u> in magazines. <u>Interviews</u> can be easier to read than novels and short stories. You can usually read one front-to-back in thirty minutes or less.

- **irony**—*n.* the use of words that mean the opposite of what you really mean. A good example is when you say "Gee, I can't wait to go to the dentist and get those cavities filled" in a sarcastic tone, when going to the dentist is obviously the last thing you want to do.

- **literal**—*adj.* the real, dictionary meaning; what a word or phrase or any kind of writing or speaking actually means. "Go jump in a lake" doesn't usually mean someone wants you to get wet. But the <u>literal</u> meaning of the phrase is exactly that—go take a leap into the nearest pond, buddy.

metaphor—*n.* figurative use of words in which a word or phrase is used to mean something other than what it usually means. As you can probably tell by now, the English language arts are all about using words in creative ways, just like the fine arts are about using paint and clay in creative ways. For a creative writer, <u>metaphors</u> are as important as paint is for an artist. In my screenplay *Pretty Dumb*, I use <u>metaphors</u> all the time. Here are a couple: Fabio was a filmmaking *machine*, churning out two to three movies a year. Pamela's career was in *overdrive*. Every part she wanted, she got. (See the definition for *simile*— it's a lot like <u>metaphor</u>.)

modify—*v.* to change in part. Adjectives and adverbs <u>modify</u> nouns and verbs. I have been <u>modifying</u> my screenplay continuously since I finished the first draft. In fact, the current version bears little resemblance to that first draft, it has undergone so many <u>modifications</u>.

mood—*n.* in English language arts, it's the general feeling created by a writer. The <u>mood</u> of a story can be sad or happy or dark or light. The writer creates the <u>mood</u> of a story by using imagery, metaphors, and all of the other writing tools. By reading a story carefully, you should be able to get a sense of its <u>mood</u>.

motivation—*n.* in English language arts, it is the reason a character does something. Tests often ask you to identify a character's <u>motivation</u>. *Example*: In my screenplay for *Pretty Dumb*, James King ends up talking about Pamela Anderson behind her back. What was James's <u>motivation</u>? To answer that, you would look for the part of the story that made James trash Pamela.

myth—*n.* a story about gods and heroes. My favorite <u>myth</u> is about the snake-haired Medusa: If you look right at her, you turn into Stone Phillips. Or do you just turn to stone? I can't remember.

narrative—*n.* a story. The <u>narrative</u> in *Pretty Dumb* follows two actresses as they angle for the starring role in a romantic comedy starring Jim Carrey.

noun—*n.* a word that names a person, place, or thing.

objective—*adj.* unaffected by emotions or other outside forces. It is impossible for me to be <u>objective</u> about my screenplay because I am so close to it. But some <u>objective</u> readers, like my sister, have told me they like it.

omniscient—*adj.* all-knowing. An <u>omniscient</u> narrator is a narrator in a story who knows everything that is going on and shares that information with the reader.

onomatopoeia—*n.* the use of words that imitate the sound they signify. *Buzz* and *splat* are good examples of <u>onomatopoeia</u>.

opinion—*n.* what someone thinks about something. *Example:* It is my <u>opinion</u> that Tom Hanks's reign as the world's most popular actor is over, and that Jim Carrey will replace him!

Whiz Quiz

Write the following sentences using metaphors:

Pam is fast.

James is confused.

Fabio likes ice cream a lot.

Whiz Tip

A good way to remember narrative is to think of the word narrator: the person who tells a story.

pace—*n.* speed. The <u>pace</u> of a story often has a lot to do with whether it reads well or not. I am trying to make sure *Pretty Dumb* goes at a very fast <u>pace</u> to keep the jokes coming one after the other.

paragraph—*n.* a distinct part of a larger written work that presents a distinct point related to the rest of the work. (<u>Paragraphs</u> usually are made up of several sentences, but a <u>paragraph</u> *can* be just one sentence.)

paraphrase—*v.* to express something using different words. Tests often ask you to <u>paraphrase</u> a story or a character's views. That just means write down what happened in the story or what a character thinks in a few sentences. I have to be able to <u>paraphrase</u> my screenplay *Pretty Dumb* in just a few words when I go try to sell it to Hollywood. Here it goes: Three days, two blonde actresses, one juicy movie role.

personification—*n.* the representation of a concept as a person. For example, I heard the golf commentator Johnny Miller say Tiger Woods is the <u>personification</u> of good sportsmanship.

persuade—*v.* to convince. Writers often try to <u>persuade</u> readers that their point of view is correct. Tests often ask you to figure out what the writer is trying to <u>persuade</u> you to think. I am <u>persuading</u> you to learn the word <u>persuade</u>. Am I being <u>persuasive</u>?

phrase—*n.* a group of related words that functions as a unit but lacks a subject, verb, or both.

plot—*n.* the events of a story. My mom thinks the <u>plot</u> of *Pretty Dumb* is, well, pretty dumb. She'll eat her words when it's a major motion picture starring Jim Carrey!

point of view—*n.* one way of looking at things. A character's <u>point of view</u> is that character's way of thinking. For example, in my screenplay *Pretty Dumb*, it is James King's <u>point of view</u> that Pamela Anderson is too old for the female lead in a Jim Carrey movie. Pamela Anderson's <u>point of view</u> is that James King is a silly supermodel who would make the Jim Carrey movie a disaster. Each tries to persuade the movie's director, Fabio, that her <u>point of view</u> is the correct one.

prefix—*n.* a few letters placed in front of a word that change its meaning. *Examples: dis-* (*dis*belief, *dis*charge); *un-* (*un*natural, *un*available).

preposition—*n.* a word that relates a noun or a pronoun to the other words in the sentence. Some popular <u>prepositions</u> are: *by*, *at*, *to*, *with*, *in*, *for*, *from*. What's that spell? BATWIFF. (You swing the batt, you whiff.) Cherish it. Remember it.

propaganda—*n.* the kind of writing that a government or group uses to get you to believe something. <u>Propaganda</u> is used all the time during wars, when one country tells its citizens that the other country is the worst country in the world. And the other

WhizTip

A good way to remember personification is to think of the word "person." You are describing an object or idea by mentioning a person.

country has <u>propaganda</u> that says the same thing about the first country. In <u>propaganda</u>, the facts aren't important—it is convincing readers that is important.

quote—*n.* exact words. *Example:* When I showed *Pretty Dumb* to a Hollywood agent he said, and I <u>quote</u>: "This screenplay will be bigger than *Star Wars*! Bigger than *Chicken Run*! Bigger than *Big*! You'll make millions!"

refrain—*n.* recurring verse or phase. *Example:* I love the refrain of Chuck Duck's latest single, *Swimming Fool*: "Don't get me wet, I just might like it! Don't get me wet, I just might like it!" It's so catchy.

relevant—*adj.* pertaining to the matter at hand. Tests often tell you to "consider the <u>relevant</u> information" before choosing your answer. You can remember what <u>relevant</u> means by thinking of the word "related." <u>Relevant</u> information is "related" to the answer.

rhyme scheme—*n.* the structure of the rhyming in a poem. One popular <u>rhyme scheme</u> is ABAB, which means the first and third lines (A) rhyme, and the second and fourth lines (B) rhyme.

root—*n.* a word or part of a word from which other words are formed. *Example:* root = *snob*. Words formed from *snob*: *snobby, snobbery, snobbish.*

run-on sentence—*n.* a sentence that continues on longer than it should, usually by using too many conjunctions.

sensory—*adj.* pertaining to the five senses (sight, smell, hearing, touch, taste). Writers often use <u>sensory</u> details to really get the reader into the story. In an early scene in *Pretty Dumb*, Fabio has terrible bad breath (halitosis!), but Pam and James ignore it because they want the part in his movie so badly.

setting—*n.* the location and time in which a story takes place.

simile—*n.* figurative language involving a comparison of unlike things using the words *like* or *as*. James is crazy *like* a fox. Pamela is smart *as* a whip. (By the way—those examples are both also clichés.)

simple sentence—*n.* a sentence containing one subject and one verb. *Example:* I eat.

suffix—*n.* a few letters placed at the end of a word that change its meaning. *Examples: -able* (believ*able*, us*able*); *-ly* (natural*ly*, common*ly*).

summarize—*v.* to create a short recap of the main points of a story. The ability to <u>summarize</u> what you read is important on English language arts tests. The best way to write a <u>summary</u> is to recap the story in the order things happened, so you don't forget anything.

symbolism—*n.* the use of an object to stand for something that can't be seen. For example, there are a lot of memorials in Washington, DC, that <u>symbolize</u> the soldiers who lost their lives in our wars. Writers use <u>symbolism</u> when they need to say some-

Briefly summarize
the last book
you read.

_____
_____
_____
_____

thing without really saying it. An example of this is when a writer <u>symbolizes</u> the passing of seasons by following a leaf as it falls from a tree and then decays on the ground, feeding the roots of the tree it fell from.

synonym—*n.* a word that means the same thing as another word. *Daring* and *adventurous* are <u>synonyms</u>. *Timid* and *cowardly* are <u>synonyms</u>. When you are writing, instead of using the same word over and over, try to use <u>synonyms</u> to change things up a little bit. So if you use the word *car* in the first sentence, use *automobile* in the second and *vehicle* in the third.

tense—*n.* in English language arts, it means the form of a verb that tells when the action takes place. *Example:* verb = chew; <u>future tense</u> = will chew; <u>past tense</u> = chewed; <u>present tense</u> = chew.

theme—*n.* the subject for a story. In school, you are often asked to write a story on a particular <u>theme</u>, like "What did you do this summer?"

thesaurus—*n.* a book of synonyms. When you are writing a paper, a <u>thesaurus</u> can help you spice things up. So, instead of using the word *great* over and over to describe yourself, you could use a thesaurus to find synonyms like *groovy, stupendous,* and *wonderful.*

timeline—*n.* a graphical representation of a chronology; a bunch of dates in chronological order on a line. <u>Timelines</u> are all over tests. Sometimes you have to write a story from a <u>timeline</u>. Sometimes you have to read a <u>timeline</u> to see what happened in what order. Here's an example from my screenplay:

Pretty Dumb: Monday

9am—Pamela meets with Fabio	1pm—Pamela and James have lunch	3pm—Pamela goes on *Extra* and trashes James	7pm—James and Pamela get in a fight at the Golden Globes
10am—James meets with Fabio		5pm—James goes on *Access Hollywood* and trashes Pamela	11pm—Fabio has a late-night meeting with a mystery actress

tone—*n.* manner of expression. *Example:* I wrote a love letter to the new girl Frieda using a very romantic <u>tone</u>. She never replied, and my heart was broken.

valid—*adj.* sound. In my screenplay *Pretty Dumb,* Fabio the director has <u>valid</u> reasons to choose James King (she is a star on the rise) and Pamela Anderson (she is a better-known blonde actress). In the end, however, Fabio chooses to put Barbra Streisand in a blonde wig. The movie is a huge hit, Fabio and Barbra and Jim Carrey all win Oscars, and an angry James King and Pamela Anderson start plotting to ruin Fabio (the plot for *Pretty Dumb II*).

verb—*n.* an action word. *Examples: bite, spit, cherish.*

WhizWords

analyze
clarify
compare
contrast
evaluate
summarize

English Language Arts

Thinking Big

Lots of times when you're taking tests, you're asked to write down a date or name that you have memorized. These kinds of test questions basically test your memory. If you remember what you memorized, you'll be just fine.

But sometimes you have to do a little more than just remember. Sometimes you have to really think about a reading passage on a test, and figure out on your own what you think and how you should write it down. These kinds of questions ask you to **analyze** a problem, **evaluate** a situation, **summarize** a story, **compare and contrast** ideas, and **clarify** your answer.

When these words appear in test questions, some kids freeze because they know a lot is expected of them—at least a lot more than just writing down a date on a history test or identifying a shape on a geometry test. A good way to stop yourself from freezing is to get used to **analyzing, evaluating, summarizing,** and **clarifying** in situations that aren't so scary.

WhizTip

One great way to build your vocabulary is to hear the words read aloud. So, until they make an audio version of this book, ask an adult to play an audio book you like when you are driving around together. Your local library probably has lots of audio books, just like mine. I personally like to listen to the *Harry Potter* books.

GETTING DEEP

In this exercise you are going to think deep about shallow things that you know a lot about. First, go back to the English Language Arts WhizWords and refresh your memory about what the "Thinking Big" words mean. Now pick a movie star, TV star, or entertainer you actually like or know a lot about. I am going to use Britney Spears as my victim, er, subject.

Write your subject at the top of the page. Now write down our six "Thinking Big" words along the left side of a piece of paper, about five lines apart. Next to each word, write down a topic relating to your victim, er, subject. Then write a short paragraph that answers the "questions" you have written. Here's mine:

Britney Spears

Analyze her album, *Oops . . . I Did It Again.*
Evaluate her singing.
Summarize why she is so popular.
Clarify her relationship with Justin Timberlake.
Compare and contrast Britney Spears and Christina Aguilera.

Once you have done this with one subject, pick another one and do it again. Keep practicing and you'll get really good at this. The more you see and use these words, the more comfortable you will get with them, and the better you'll do on your tests.

On the Test

Which is the best summary of this passage?

WhizWords

analogy
dialect
figurative language
flashback
foreshadow
imagery
irony
metaphor
mood
personification
simile
symbolism
tone

English Language Arts
Writers' Tools

Good writers know how to use all sorts of tools to keep readers' eyes glued to the page (that's a **metaphor**, by the way). Some writers are so good at it, you just can't stop reading. I keep a flashlight under my bed for nights when my parents tell me to turn out my light and go to sleep, but I just can't stop reading. Good writers make writing look easy, so you don't notice all of the tools they are using.

But on tests, it's important to be able to pick out the tools writers use. Lots of reading questions on tests ask you to identify things like **metaphors, symbolism**, and **analogies**—basically all of the words that I have listed at the top of this page. The only way to learn how to find all of these things is to practice finding them in the stories you read every day.

IDENTIFYING A WRITER'S TOOLS

You are going to have to do a little hunting and gathering for this exercise. I want you to go through your house and get on the internet and find examples of the following types of stories:

> Newspaper—sports story
> Magazine—fashion story
> Internet (print one out)—movie review
> Newspaper—article from the editorial page
> Internet (print one out)—piece of short fiction
> Magazine—celebrity profile
> Newspaper—political story

Gather these up in one place. Now, over the next week, I want you to read one of these stories every day and:

> 1. Underline the writer's tools.
> 2. Write the writer's tools in the margin.

There probably won't be enough room in the margins for some of these. If there isn't, you can write down the writer's tools you identify on Post-it Notes and stick them to the story.

English Language Arts
Adverbs and Adjectives

Imagine a world made up of only nouns and verbs. Actors would be . . . just actors. Not *terrible* actors, not *handsome* actors, not *overpaid* actors . . . just actors. Singers would be . . . just singers. Not *gorgeous* singers or *overproduced* singers or singers with voices that only a mother could love. Just . . . singers.

Luckily we have **adverbs** and **adjectives**, the words that make life special! The Texas Rangers' Alex Rodriguez is the best shortstop in the league with a *sweet* swing, *nimble* feet and *soft* hands. The Rangers are *perennial* challengers for the American League pennant, with *incredible* talent and *limitless* potential.

Yes, **adjectives** and **adverbs**, the simple modifiers of verbs, nouns and other **adjectives** and **adverbs**, give writing its spice. So it is very important to use them when you write. It makes your writing more interesting to read, which gets you better grades on your papers and writing tests. All good things, wouldn't you say?

WRITING YOUR AUTOBIOGRAPHY

If you don't believe me, let me prove it. I want you to try to describe your own life without adjectives and adverbs. Then I want you to describe your life WITH adjectives and adverbs—as many as you can possibly think of.

That's right—it's autobiography time. Grab a pencil and paper. Start by filling out this general outline. Write down three events in each age bracket you will write about in your own journal or notebook. Stuff like losing your first tooth, learning to swim, moving to a new town, joining the basketball team—events that are memorable and important to you.

Age

0 – 4
_____

5 – 8
_____

9 – present
_____

Now write two versions of your autobiography: 1) using no adverbs or adjectives; 2) using as many adverbs and adjectives as you can think of. Underline the adjectives and adverbs in the second version when you are done. I have provided you with a few adjectives and adverbs that you can use if you get stumped.

Adjectives and
adverbs for your
autobiography:
goofy
fast
unbelievable
slow
smelly
late
first
early
straight
green
gawky
crazy
funny
laughable
smart
right
heavenly
regrettable

Chapter 2
Social Studies

Related Word

abolish—v. to get rid of.

abolitionist—*n.* someone who fought against slavery. When this country had slavery, there were a bunch of <u>abolitionists</u> trying to free the slaves. Some gave speeches, some ran the underground railroad—all of the <u>abolitionists</u> were working to stop a terrible system.

acculturation—*n.* the modification of one culture when it is exposed to another. When people from other countries emigrate to America, they go through a process of <u>acculturation</u> in which their "home" culture is influenced by American culture.

adapt—*v.* to change in response to new circumstances. The word is often used to describe how people and animals <u>adapt</u> as the environment changes. For example, animals <u>adapt</u> to colder climates by growing thicker fur, building warm shelters, and storing food.

adversary—*n.* the enemy! John F. Kennedy's <u>adversary</u> in the 1960 presidential election was Richard Nixon.

aggressor—*n.* the person or country who attacks first. Germany was the <u>aggressor</u> in World War II.

Antonym

industrial—adj. pertaining to an economy based on industry (building things).

agrarian—*adj.* pertaining to a culture or economy based on farming and agriculture. The U.S. went from an <u>agrarian</u> economy in the 1800s to an industrial economy in the 1900s. Now there are hardly any farmers left.

allegiance—*n.* a deep commitment to something, like your country or your family. Of course, we have all pledged <u>allegiance</u> to the flag in school.

alliance—*n.* an association of people or nations coming together to achieve a common goal. Think of the TV show *Survivor*—the players try to form <u>alliances</u> to protect themselves from getting voted off the show.

Whiz Fact

The first ten amendments to the U.S. Constitution are called the Bill of Rights.

amendment—*n.* a change that corrects or improves something. We have had 27 <u>amendments</u> to our Constitution since it was adopted in 1789.

antebellum—*adj.* of the period prior to the Civil War. It's most often used in the phrase "the <u>antebellum</u> South," to describe the South before the Civil War. Think about the movie *Gone With the Wind*: southern gentlemen, women in hoop skirts, plantations—and slaves.

antitrust—*adj.* opposing business monopolies. <u>Antitrust</u> laws in the United States are supposed to keep one company from controlling an entire industry.

artifact—*n.* a tool or weapon from an ancient culture. I actually found an <u>artifact</u> myself when my family went camping in the Adirondack Mountains last year. I was digging for worms to use for fish bait when I found an arrowhead!

assimilate—*v.* to make similar or to absorb into a system or culture. This word is often used when discussing how immigrants are absorbed into American culture. <u>Assimilation</u> is a complex process. Immigrants come here with their own customs. They want to keep some customs, but they also need to adopt some American customs. So the country <u>assimilates</u> them, but it is never easy.

authority—*n.* power; the person with the power. As the captain of my soccer team, I have the <u>authority</u> to talk to the referees. Nobody else except Coach Munster has that <u>authority</u>.

barrier—*n.* a block; an obstacle. High tariffs are often cited as a <u>barrier</u> to free trade among countries.

barter—*v.* to pay for stuff with other stuff, instead of with money. *Example*: When we got to the field late, Coach Munster <u>bartered</u> with the opposing team for an extra ten minutes of warm-up time. In return they got all of our new water bottles.

benevolent—*adj.* kind; caring. Often used when talking about a "<u>benevolent</u> dictator," which means the dictator has total power, but he uses it for good, not evil. Superman would be a <u>benevolent</u> dictator.

bias—*n.* prejudice. It usually means having a negative attitude about someone for a reason that doesn't make any sense, like gender or skin color. That is <u>bias</u>, or prejudice.

DOUBLE MEANING
assimilate—v.
to break food
down into its
nutrients and
absorb it
(science).

**One way to
remember
benevolent is to
imagine a nice
person named Ben,
like Ben Franklin
or Ben Affleck.**

Social Studies

● **boom and bust economy**—*n.* a kind of economy where things go incredibly well for a while, then crash and go incredibly poorly from there on out. It is most often used to describe the California Gold Rush in the 1800s, when everyone flocked to California for the <u>boom</u>, but once everyone was there and all of the gold had been mined, it all went <u>bust</u>.

● **boycott**—*v.* to refuse to have dealings with a company or country because you disagree with something it does. It is a peaceful way to protest. Instead of picketing or doing something violent, people can <u>boycott</u>. Martin Luther King Jr. convinced black people to <u>boycott</u> the Montgomery, Alabama, bus system to protest segregation on the buses. That meant no black people would ride the buses, which meant the buses lost a lot of money. So then they had to pay attention to what Martin Luther King Jr. said, or they would go out of business.

● **Buddhism**—*proper noun.* a religious doctrine that says life and suffering go hand-in-hand, and that only by renouncing your self and your senses can you be freed from suffering and existence.

● **buffalo soldier**—*n.* a black soldier who fought against the Native Americans during westward expansion. The Native Americans gave them the name <u>buffalo soldiers</u> because of the courage they displayed in battle.

DOUBLE MEANING
capital—n.
the city where a state or nation's government is located.

● **capital**—*n.* in economics, it means the wealth used to create more wealth. Basically, <u>capital</u> is money or property. If you were going to start a dot-com company, you would need some <u>capital</u> to start with—that includes money to pay for your staff, a place to work, and some computers to work on.

● **capitalism**—*n.* an economic system in which the means or production are privately owned and goods and services are sold in a free market. The United States has a <u>capitalist</u> economy.

WhizFact

The term carpetbagger was used to describe Northerners who moved South after the Civil War with nothing but the contents of their carpet-bags (suitcases) to take advantage of the post-war chaos to enter politics.

● **carpetbagger**—*n.* a politician who runs for office in a state she is not from. Hilary Clinton was called a <u>carpetbagger</u> when she ran for Senate in New York in 2000, even though she was from Illinois and had never lived in New York before. (It didn't matter—she won anyway!)

● **censorship**—*n.* restriction on what someone can say or do. Although the First Amendment to the Constitution protects our right to freedom of speech, television shows are <u>censored</u>, movies are <u>censored</u>, and songs are <u>censored</u>. It happens every day in this country—usually to protect young people from adult language and situations. Many artists and performers are frustrated by <u>censorship</u> in the United States. Some countries, however, <u>censor</u> everyone on what they can say anywhere, anytime. This type of <u>censorship</u> is used to control people and prevent them from complaining about the government.

centralized—*adj.* focused in one person or area. In social studies, the word is usually used to describe governments. A <u>centralized</u> government gives a lot of power to one person or group of people—like a king or a single ruling party. A <u>decentralized</u> government spreads that power out to a lot of people or groups of people.

checks and balances—*n.* when talking about the U.S. government, it is the system of government branches that each limit one another's power. So the president can do some things, but Congress has a say in what he does. Same with Congress—it can do some things, but the president also has a say. The judiciary branch—the courts—has a say in everything, too, and Congress and the president have a say in who gets to be a judge.

Christianity—*proper noun.* a monotheistic religion based on the teachings of Jesus Christ, who taught, among other things, to love thy neighbor as thyself. Its sacred text is the Bible.

chronological—*adj.* in time order.

circumstances—*n.* the conditions and facts surrounding an event. In a recent pie-eating contest, <u>circumstances</u> worked against me. The pies placed before me were all giants, while my competitors' pies were normal sized. Oh well— sometimes you can't control your <u>circumstances</u>.

civic—*adj.* relating to your city or town. This word is sometimes used when discussing your role as a citizen. People often say "It's your <u>civic</u> duty to vote." That just means that as a member of a community, you should take part in what is going on there.

civil disobedience—*n.* a kind of protest where someone refuses to obey civil laws because she doesn't believe in them. <u>Civil disobedience</u> is almost always nonviolent. Martin Luther King Jr. organized sit-ins to protest "whites-only" restaurants. Black people would simply sit at a table and not leave until the cops came and arrested them.

civil rights—*n.* the rights that are due you simply by being a citizen of this country. Martin Luther King Jr. organized acts of civil disobedience because blacks had unequal <u>civil rights</u> from whites.

coerce—*v.* to force someone to do something by threatening him. I was <u>coerced</u> into babysitting for my sister last weekend— my dad said if I didn't, I wouldn't get the new PlayStation— ever! You may have heard about the <u>Coercive Acts</u> that England forced on the American colonies (called the Intolerable Acts by the colonists) after the Boston Tea Party.

colonize—*v.* to establish a culture in a foreign land by putting some citizens there. It often results in those citizens taking over that foreign land. It's not a very nice thing to do, but it

On the Test

Based on the information from the passage, give three examples of a citizen's **civic** responsibilities.

The American writer Henry David Thoreau coined the term civil disobedience in the late 19th century.

Social Studies

has been a common practice for many countries, including the United States.

commerce—*n.* the act of buying and selling things. When you go to Wal-Mart and buy a notebook, you are engaging in com<u>merce</u>, and so is Wal-Mart.

commodity—*n.* something that is bought or sold. Like a notebook or a car or a ton of grain. They are all <u>commodities</u>.

communism—*n.* a system where the people own the factories, farms, and other property. At least that is the <u>communist</u> ideal. In most <u>communist</u> countries so far—like Cuba and the old Soviet Union—the government "owns" the property and most of the people have little say in how everything is run.

competition—*n.* in economics, rivalry between two businesses for the same consumers. Fruity Pebbles and Alpha-Bits are engaged in ferocious <u>competition</u> to be my cereal of choice.

compromise—*n.* a settlement where each side gives up something. So if you want to watch TV after dinner but your dad wants you to wash the dishes, a <u>compromise</u> would be watching TV, and then washing the dishes afterward.

concession—*n.* something that is given up. When I wanted to switch bedrooms with my big sister Esther, I offered a series of <u>concessions</u>: I would do her laundry, I would bow low whenever she came into a room, and I would give her my dessert for a whole year. She didn't budge.

Congress *proper noun*—the U.S. Senate and House of Representatives. *Note*: <u>Congress</u> is one of the three branches of the U.S. government.

consensus—*n.* general agreement. After my big sister Esther refused to switch bedrooms with me, I tried to form a <u>consensus</u> among the rest of my family (parents, grandparents, cousins, uncles, aunts) that I deserved her room. While I succeeded, and they agreed with me, she still wouldn't budge.

consequence—*n.* the result of something that happened. As a parent or teacher must have told you at some point in your life, there are <u>consequences</u> for your actions. In history class, the word is usually used when talking about something bad that happened, like Japan bombing Pearl Harbor (<u>consequence</u>: the U.S. joined the war) or the Watergate scandal (<u>consequence</u>: Nixon resigned). But <u>consequences</u> can also stem from positive events.

constitution—*n.* the laws that govern a group of people, usually a country or state. The U.S. <u>Constitution</u> has in it the basic laws that we follow in this country.

consumption—*n.* to use up consumer goods and services. When I <u>consume</u> the Fruity Pebbles my mom bought at the grocery store, I am involved in the <u>consumption</u> of goods.

controversy—*n.* a situation where two sides have opposing views, and people have a hard time figuring out who is right. There was a huge <u>controversy</u> at my school last year when my friend Lamonte refused to wear the new uniform—and his parents agreed with him! The principal called an assembly, Lamonte's parents were in and out of school almost every day, Lamonte was suspended, and it was in the newspaper!

corrupt—*adj.* marked by dishonesty. The history of the United States is filled with <u>corrupt</u> politicians—politicians who took bribes to get laws passed.

cost-benefit analysis—*n.* analyzing the price of something versus the good it does. I did a <u>cost-benefit analysis</u> on my Skittles consumption and came to the conclusion that the benefits (yummy good times) far outweighed the cost ($.79 a pack).

covenant—*n.* a binding agreement; a compact. It's basically promising something, cross-your-heart, hope to die, stick a needle in your eye. A serious promise.

cuneiform—*n.* wedge-shaped characters used in several forms of ancient writing.

currency—*n.* a country's money. Our <u>currency</u> is dollars, the British use pounds, and the Japanese use yen.

debate—*v.* to argue. During the last presidential election my parents were both glued to the television for the presidential <u>debates</u>, which meant I couldn't use my PlayStation. Needless to say, I was not happy.

democracy—*n.* a government where the people hold the power. We have a representative <u>democracy</u>, which means we elect representatives to do what we, the people, want them to do.

despotism—*n.* rule by a despot, someone who has absolute power and can do whatever he wants. Hitler was a <u>despot</u> in Germany. Saddam Hussein is a <u>despot</u> in Iraq. There are still lots of <u>despots</u> around the world.

detente—*n.* the relaxing of tensions between nations. After the Cold War between the United States and Russia ended in the 1990s, the countries have been enjoying a period of <u>detente</u>.

deter—*v.* to prevent; to stop. My mom doesn't understand why Britney Spears' mom doesn't try to <u>deter</u> her from wearing those skimpy outfits.

diffuse—*v.* in social science, the spreading of one culture throughout another. When people from another country immigrate to the United States, they often gradually <u>diffuse</u> through the country, spreading out through the land.

WhizFact

The Mayflower Compact was a covenant signed by the forty-one male passengers on the Mayflower, saying they would stick together.

Social Studies

diplomat—*n.* a person who represents her country while living in another country. Most countries have <u>diplomats</u> in other countries, so if something happens, say, in Mexico, the United States' <u>diplomat</u> in Mexico can make sure the United States' interests are kept in mind.

discriminate—*v.* to treat someone badly for unfair reasons. Black people have been <u>discriminated</u> against a lot in our country. Even my favorite sport, baseball, <u>discriminated</u> against black people until 1947, when Jackie Robinson became the first black man in the Major Leagues. And racial <u>discrimination</u> still exists—there may be tons of black players, but there are hardly any black managers.

dissent—*n.* disagreement. In America, you have the right to register your <u>dissent</u>, no matter what you think. It's called freedom of speech. My friend Lamonte's parents had every right to register their <u>dissent</u> with the school's dress code. They lost—Lamonte had to wear the uniform like the rest of us, but they still had the right to disagree.

distribution—*n.* the act of marketing and supplying goods and services to consumers. Snags in <u>distribution</u> caused our grocery store to be without Alpha-Bits for more than two weeks. That's when I started eating Fruity Pebbles for breakfast.

diversity—*n.* variety. In history, the word is usually used to talk about the <u>diversity</u> of opinions (lots of different opinions) and the <u>diversity</u> of cultures (lots of different cultures) that make up America. Some call our <u>diversity</u> a melting pot, some call it a quilt—the point is, we have a very <u>diverse</u> society.

domestic—*adj.* having to do with home. In social science, you may hear the phrase "<u>domestic</u> affairs"—that refers to issues within a country, not in other countries.

dominate—*v.* to take precedence; to be most important. Combining the definition above with this one, you may have heard of "domestic affairs <u>dominating</u> Congress" or something along those lines. That means issues close to home are taking up most of the time and effort in Congress. Different issues tend to <u>dominate</u> in our culture, depending on all sorts of things: war and peace, the economy, the rights of people being respected or abused. All of these issues have <u>dominated</u> at one time or another.

due process—*n.* the established way our court system works. The phrase "You have a right to <u>due process</u>" is very important in this country. It means no matter who you are, you get treated the same—and fairly—in our court system.

economy—*n.* the combination of goods, services, and people and how they all work together to survive. We have a market economy, which means the laws of supply and demand determine who makes and gets what. The other kind of economy is a command economy, where a government determines (commands) who makes and gets what. China has a command economy.

eloquent—*adj.* good at public speaking. If you are president, it helps to be eloquent, since you have to make so many speeches all the time. John F. Kennedy was an eloquent speaker; so were Ronald Reagan and Bill Clinton. But I think the most eloquent speaker I know is the Rock on WWF. That guy can really hold an audience!

emancipation—*n.* the act of gaining freedom. Our emancipation from England and the emancipation of slaves in our country are two pivotal moments in our history.

embargo—*n.* the prohibition of goods from entering or leaving a country. After the Gulf War, the United States put an oil embargo on Iraq so they couldn't sell oil to anyone anymore.

emigrate—*v.* to leave one's home country for another. This country is made up of millions of people who have emigrated from distant lands to find opportunity here.

enforce—*v.* to make sure something takes place. Often used in the phrases "enforce our laws" and "enforce our borders." It just means if we say we are going to do something, we will do it. My parents enforce their home rules by grounding me and taking away things when I break the rules.

enlighten—*v.* to inform. My big sister Esther enlightened me about why I would never get her room: she is bigger, stronger, and older, and couldn't care less how small my room is.

entrepreneur—*n.* someone who takes business risks in a capitalist economy. It can be someone who bets that if she is right about a business venture, she will get rich. Entrepreneurs start most of the new companies in our country every year, betting each business will succeed. Steve Jobs was an entrepreneur when he started Apple Computer in his garage in the 1970s. Martha Stewart took an ability to make pretty doilies and turned it into a multi-million dollar home-decoration empire. Smart!

ethics—*n.* moral rules that govern individuals or groups. For example, medical ethics start with the promise that doctors "First, do no harm." That means a doctor must not make a patient any sicker than he already is.

ethnic—*adj.* pertaining to a particular national, religious, racial, or cultural group.

ethnocentrism—*n.* belief that one's ethnic group is better than all the others. Ethnocentrism is a leading cause of wars.

executive branch—*n.* the branch of government that administers

Whiz Tip

The U.S. is called "the land of the free," so emancipation (freedom) is probably our most important ideal. That means you are lucky—but it also means lots of test questions on the subject.

Whiz Tip

Think of "using force" to remember the word enforce.

the country. The president is the head of the <u>executive branch</u>.

expansionism—*n*. the policy of taking over additional land and countries. The United States had an <u>expansionist</u> policy, particularly in the 19th century. That's how it grew from thirteen to fifty states so quickly.

export—*n*. 1) goods sent to another country to be sold. 2) *v*. to send goods to another country.

fascism—*n*. a government with a ruthless dictator, centralized control, and nationalist tendencies. Hitler was a <u>fascist</u>. So was Mussolini. The Allied Powers fought <u>fascism</u> in World War II and won. It's all my great-grandfather talks about!

federalism—*n*. a government with separate states that are united under one larger government. The United States (get it—*united* states) is a <u>federalist</u> system. Alexander Hamilton was an advocate of <u>federalism</u>.

feminism—*n*. a movement committed to getting women the same rights and opportunities as men. Women make less money than men for the same work, and our society treats them differently in many ways. <u>Feminists</u> are out to change that so everyone is equal.

fertile—*adj*. capable of sustaining crops. America is an incredibly <u>fertile</u> country, growing much more food than Americans could ever consume.

fiscal—*adj*. pertaining to finances. This word is often used in the phrase "<u>fiscal</u> policy." <u>Fiscal</u> policy is a government's plan for how it gets and spends its money.

forfeit—*v*. to give up; to hand over. When someone commits a crime and goes to jail, he <u>forfeits</u> a lot of his rights as a citizen, like the freedom to walk around and go wherever he wants. If your baseball team doesn't show up for a game, it <u>forfeits</u> the game and loses automatically. That happened to my team when our bus broke down.

fortification—*n*. a defensive structure like a fort or a wall. The Great Wall of China is a good example of a <u>fortification</u>. (It's also the only man-made structure you can see from outer space!)

free enterprise—*n*. an economic system in which businesses can try to make a profit without the government getting in their way with lots of regulations. The United States has a <u>free enterprise</u> system.

frontier—*n*. an area of land where people don't live yet; the great unknown. The United States was once just a few states on the East Coast with a great <u>frontier</u> to its west that still "belonged" to the Native Americans. If you're a *Star Trek* fan,

Whiz Fact

Gloria Steinem and Betty Friedan are famous modern feminists. Elizabeth Cady Stanton is a famous suffragette —a woman who fought for women's right to vote in the early 20th century (see definition for suffrage).

you've heard William Shatner say these words a million times: "Space—the final <u>frontier</u> . . . . These are the voyages of the Starship Enterprise. Its five-year mission: to explore strange new worlds, to seek out new life and new civilizations, to boldly go where no man has gone before." That's exactly how the pioneers felt when they packed up their covered wagons and headed out West.

fundamental—*adj.* basic. In this country we have certain <u>fundamental</u> rights—the rights to life, liberty, and the pursuit of happiness. Maybe you've heard of these somewhere?

futile—*adj.* useless. Lots of times people will tell you not to try, that trying is <u>futile</u>. My sister keeps saying that about me trying to get her bedroom.

genocide—*n.* the planned killing of an entire group of people. Hitler's Nazis practiced <u>genocide</u> against the Jews. The United States practiced <u>genocide</u> against Native Americans.

grievance—*n.* complaint. The colonists had a list of <u>grievances</u> against mother England, the biggest of which was they were getting taxed a lot. I have a list of <u>grievances</u> I gave to my mother last week, the biggest of which was my allowance needs to be higher. The colonists rebelled. I hope my mom gets the hint.

hazardous—*adj.* dangerous. You've probably seen this word in ads for cigarettes: "CAUTION: Cigarette smoking may be <u>hazardous</u> to your health." Being an early colonist was also definitely <u>hazardous</u> to one's health.

idealist—*n.* one who is more influenced by ideals than by practicalities. An <u>idealist</u> wants to do what is right no matter how hard or impractical it may be.

immigration—*n.* the act of coming from a foreign country to live in a new country. America has grown in population over the years mainly due to <u>immigration</u>. The country practically begged people to <u>immigrate</u> here so it could push west over the frontier and fill up all of its land with new citizens.

impartial—*adj.* fair. Judges and juries are supposed to be <u>impartial</u>. That means they just go by the facts. Like Judge Judy on TV—she is an <u>impartial</u> judge who listens to all the facts, then she reams the person who is guilty.

impeachment—*n.* charging an elected official with doing something wrong. President Clinton was <u>impeached</u> a few years ago. It was only the second time in the history of the country a president was <u>impeached</u>. Clinton's <u>impeachment</u> hearings dominated the news for weeks.

imperialism—*n.* rule by an empire. A few hundred years ago, <u>imperialism</u> was the way to go. There was the Roman Empire,

List three things you once thought were futile:

1. _____
2. _____
3. _____

On the Test
How many immigrants came to the United States between 1820 and 1829?

Who was the first president to be impeached? Hint: It wasn't Bill Clinton.

_____

Social Studies

the Spanish Empire, and the German Empire. These <u>imperial</u> governments would go out and conquer a bunch of countries so they could expand their empires. Of course America was part of the British Empire—<u>imperial</u> Britain—at one point.

import—*n.* 1) goods made in and sent by another country to be sold in this country. My parents' car is an <u>import</u>: it's a Honda Accord made in Japan. 2) *v.* to bring into one's country goods for sale.

inalienable—*adj.* unable to be taken away; unable to be separated from. Most often linked to Americans' <u>inalienable</u> rights of life, liberty, and the pursuit of happiness. One way to remember this word is to think about the word "alien." Space aliens are beings from other planets. So something that is <u>INalienable</u> is something that is NOT something from another planet.

inaugurate—*v.* to have a ceremony where a politician gets installed in office. George W. Bush was <u>inaugurated</u> in 2001 after a bitter election battle against Al Gore.

incentive—*n.* reward. Dad gave me a great <u>incentive</u> for mowing the lawn early Saturday morning: If I finished by noon, we could go to the car show at the convention center!

indigenous—*adj.* native. The people who are originally from a country are called the country's <u>indigenous</u> people. Native Americans are <u>indigenous</u> to North America—everyone else who lives in this country came here from somewhere else or is descended from someone who did.

industrialism—*n.* an economic system where big industries are most important. <u>Industrialism</u> dominated the United States in the 20th century.

inevitable—*adj.* going to happen; unavoidable. It is <u>inevitable</u> that you are going to have to take tests, so you might as well just get used to them. When something is unavoidable, my grandfather always says, "It's as <u>inevitable</u> as death and taxes."

influence—*n.* the power to change something. The United States has incredible <u>influence</u> around the world due to our economic and military might. In 1936, a man named Dale Carnegie wrote a book called *How to Win Friends and <u>Influence</u> People*, and it became one of the best-selling books of all time because, well, that's what everyone wants, right?

inhabitant—*n.* someone who lives in a particular location. Prince Charles is an <u>inhabitant</u> of England.

Related **Word**

innovate—**v.**
**to introduce
something new.**

innovation—*n.* a brand new way of doing something or a new device that is better than it used to be. The electric guitar was an <u>innovation</u> that allowed bands to play louder. Before the electric guitar, the only way to play loud was on an acoustic guitar aimed at a microphone. Boring!

instability—*n.* the state of being unsteady and insecure. When things are up in the air, when they can go one way or the other—that is <u>instability</u>. *Example*: There is <u>instability</u> on a baseball team when the players don't like the manager and the manager doesn't like the players. Who is right—the players who say the manager is stupid or the manager who says the players are terrible? Who do you side with? All these questions lead to <u>instability</u>. It's the same with a country when there is <u>instability</u>. Usually, there is <u>instability</u> when there is a change in leaders. Maybe the army liked the old leader better, so they won't listen to the new leader. That leads to <u>instability</u>.

insurgent—*n.* a person who revolts against authority. When you watch newscasters, you may hear them talk about "rebel <u>insurgents</u>" in other countries, and then show some guys with machine guns running around in the woods fighting against government forces.

insurrection—*n.* revolt against the people in charge. The word is used in the Declaration of Independence to describe the King of England's treatment of the colonies: "He has excited domestic <u>insurrections</u> amongst us." That means the colonists thought the king was turning them against each other.

integration—*n.* the creation of one group by combining different groups; having people of all different races living together instead of apart. Our country was segregated—white people and black people were separated from each other—until the 1950s and 1960s, when segregation was made illegal. Now we are an <u>integrated</u> society—people of all races are allowed to live side by side.

integrity—*n.* honesty; trustworthiness. People who do what they say they are going to do have <u>integrity</u>. People who lie do not have <u>integrity</u>. I think Justin Timberlake has <u>integrity</u> for staying with 'N Sync so long, even though he could have gone solo years ago and made millions.

interdependent—*adj.* relying or counting on each other. Countries are getting more and more <u>interdependent</u>. Lots of countries rely on us for corn; we rely on lots of countries for oil; and everyone relies on France for French fries.

intervene—*v.* to butt in. I had to <u>intervene</u> on the playground last week when my friend Lamonte and that jerk Frankie got into a fight. I was able to keep them apart until the teacher came.

intolerant—*adj.* unable to accept views one doesn't agree with. There are lots of <u>intolerant</u> people in the world—people who don't like other people just because they are different. Don't be <u>intolerant</u>. It will just make you mean.

invasion—*n.* an attack on another country and the taking over

Whiz Fact

Famous **insurgents** include civil rights leader Martin Luther King Jr., our third president Thomas Jefferson, and the poet Allen Ginsberg. They all went against authority.

Think of the word "depend" to remember interdependent.

of their land. The D-Day <u>invasion</u> of Normandy in World War II in 1944 is the largest, and one of the most famous, <u>invasions</u> ever. The Allied forces caught the Germans by surprise and ended up driving them out of France.

Islam—*proper noun.* a monotheistic religion based on the teachings of the prophet Mohammad. Its sacred text is the Quran (also spelled *Koran*).

isolate—*v.* to separate from everything else. When I was in kindergarten, I was a big spaz. Sometimes I got so hyper my teacher had to <u>isolate</u> me at nap time—she put up big dividers so I couldn't see the rest of the kids and they couldn't see me.

judicial branch—*n.* the country's court system. One of three branches of the U.S. government, the <u>judicial branch</u> interprets the laws and hands down punishments.

jurisdiction—*n.* an area of authority. The word <u>jurisdiction</u> is often used to talk about the courts having <u>jurisdiction</u> over a case. That means the case happened in a court's physical area. So if someone robbed someone in Suffolk County, the case would be tried in the <u>jurisdiction</u> of Suffolk County.

laissez-faire—*adj.* favoring an economic doctrine that opposes government regulations. <u>Laissez-faire</u> economists think markets solve problems best, not governments.

lame duck—*n.* a politician who has some time left in her term, but her replacement has already been elected. So she is still doing her job, but she has already been voted out. That means she has no power, and she's basically just keeping the seat warm for her successor.

legislation—*n.* proposed laws. In the U.S. government, Congress writes and votes on <u>legislation</u>.

legislative branch—*n.* the branch of government that writes the laws. The U.S. has a bicameral <u>legislative branch</u> made up of the House of Representatives and the Senate.

limit—*n.* the end; the most; the end of the line. My <u>limit</u> on chicken wings is 28. I have never eaten more than 28, although I have tried many times.

loyalist—*n.* someone who is loyal to a leader or government. <u>Loyalists</u> who lived in the American colonies were against the colonies breaking from mother England.

mandate—*n.* the right to do something. In elections, when voters pick someone overwhelmingly, that politician has a <u>mandate</u>. That means the voters have told him—with their votes—that he can do what he wants because they agree with his plan. When a politician wins in a landslide, he has a <u>mandate</u> from the voters. When there is a close election (like when George W. Bush barely beat Al Gore in 2000), there is not a <u>mandate</u> because lots of

Whiz Tip

To remember jurisdiction, think of the word "jury." A case's jurisdiction is wherever a jury would be seated to try the case.

Whiz Quiz

Go to *www.house.gov* and find a piece of legislation Congress is working on now.

Related Word

landslide—n. an election won by a huge margin.

people voted for the guy who lost.

manifest destiny—*n.* a policy of imperialist expansion that says a country can take over another country because God says so. Imperialist countries like England took over other countries using this concept of <u>manifest destiny</u>. The United States took over lots of its western lands by using this concept of <u>manifest destiny</u>. <u>Manifest destiny</u> is bad. It's basically just an excuse to take over a country.

mercenary—*n.* a professional soldier. <u>Mercenaries</u> fight for whomever pays them to fight. There's even a magazine for <u>mercenaries</u> called *Soldier of Fortune*. Get it? They *soldier* so they can make a *fortune*.

migration—*n.* the movement from one place to another. In the past twenty years, there has been a <u>migration</u> of people in this country from cold states like Maine to warm states like Georgia.

militant—*adj.* combative; warring. Some countries have <u>militant</u> histories, ours included.

misconception—*n.* an incorrect assumption. My sister is under the <u>misconception</u> that I have given up trying to trade my tiny bedroom for her big bedroom. I have many more tricks up my sleeves.

moderate—*adj.* not extreme. <u>Moderate</u> temperatures are not too hot and not too cold. <u>Moderate</u> politicians are not too liberal and not too conservative.

monotheistic—*adj.* believing in one god. Christianity and Islam are <u>monotheistic</u> religions. There are also polytheistic religions, like Hinduism, that worship many gods.

mutual—*adj.* shared in common between two people, things, or groups. When something is done for <u>mutual</u> benefit, that means they both benefit. When Justin Timberlake and Britney Spears are seen in public together, they <u>mutually</u> benefit. All of her fans start to like him, and all of his fans start to like her.

nationalism—*n.* loyalty to one's country. <u>Nationalism</u> is a good thing when it means you really like your country and are proud of it. <u>Nationalism</u> is a bad thing when it means you really like your country but hate all the other countries. Most often these days, when you hear about <u>nationalism</u>, it's when one country is beating up on another one out of a feeling of <u>nationalism</u>.

naturalization—*n.* the granting of citizenship to someone. The word is most often used when discussing the INS—the Immigration and <u>Naturalization</u> Service. That is the agency that helps people immigrate to this country and become citizens. A <u>naturalized</u> citizen is someone who immigrated here and became

DOUBLE MEANING
moderate—v.
to manage a group of people who have different views.

The scientist Albert Einstein once said "Nationalism is an infantile sickness. It is the measles of the human race."

Social Studies

a citizen later.

negotiate—*v.* to discuss something with the goal of reaching an agreement. Throughout history there have basically been two ways to solve disagreements—to fight or to <u>negotiate</u>. <u>Negotiating</u> is better, because nobody gets hurt.

neutral—*adj.* not taking sides. Lots of times, when two countries go to war, other countries remain <u>neutral</u>. That means they aren't taking sides in the war—they are staying out of it. The United States was <u>neutral</u> in World War II until Japan bombed Pearl Harbor.

nullify—*v.* to void; to take something back. Sometimes, after an agreement has been negotiated, something happens and the agreement gets <u>nullified</u>. That means all the negotiating was wasted, because the agreement that was reached doesn't count. It happens all the time in baseball when a team is trying to make a trade, but the trade gets <u>nullified</u> when one of the players doesn't pass his physical.

Whiz Quiz

Name your
favorite team's
main opposition:

_____

opposition—*n.* someone who is against someone else. It looks like Britney Spears's main <u>opposition</u> for the rest of her career is going to be rival singer Christina Aguilera. Go Britney!

oppress—*v.* to keep somebody down. This country has a history of <u>oppressing</u> black people and women. That <u>oppression</u> isn't nearly as bad now as it used to be.

partisan—*n.* a supporter of a political party; a supporter of a cause. You have probably heard of "<u>partisan</u> politics" in Washington, DC. That means our two major political parties—the Democrats and Republicans—are more interested in getting their way than getting something done. Being a <u>partisan</u>—a supporter of their party—is more important than doing what they were elected to do.

patriotism—*n.* love of one's country. *Note*: <u>Patriotism</u> is similar to nationalism, but nationalism has a negative connotation because it means one thinks less of other countries, as well.

persecute—*v.* to oppress. The Nazis <u>persecuted</u> Jews in World War II. The Romans <u>persecuted</u> Christians for hundreds of years. European colonists <u>persecuted</u> Native Americans for hundreds of years. Unfortunately, the history of mankind is filled with <u>persecution</u>.

petition—*n.* a formal request to a government or another authority. You have probably signed a <u>petition</u> at some point in your life. Last year I signed a <u>petition</u> to end the dress code at my school, but it didn't work—we still have a dress code!

pivotal—*adj.* the most important. The <u>pivotal</u> moment of my last baseball game was when the other team had the bases loaded and I struck out their best hitter. That's what I call <u>pivotal</u>.

polarize—*v.* to cause two groups to focus on their differences. The issue of slavery <u>polarized</u> the United States in the 1800s.

populism—*n.* a political philosophy that puts the needs of the "common people" first. <u>Populist</u> politicians usually talk about having the rich pay their fair share in taxes and redistributing the nation's wealth to the poorer people.

prejudice—*n.* an opinion reached about a person or event without knowing the facts. You can break the word down into its components: *pre* and *judge*. <u>Prejudice</u> is *prejudging* a person or situation. It is often used when discussing racial <u>prejudice</u>.

preservation—*n.* protection from destruction. This word is often used when people are talking about <u>preserving</u> old buildings in their town (historic <u>preservation</u>) and when people are talking about preserving the environment (environmental <u>preservation</u>).

Related Word
self-preservation—
**n. the act of doing
things that help
you survive.**

primary source—*n.* a first-hand record of an event. I was doing a report on how the Hall of Fame pitcher Cy Young got so good. Some of my <u>primary sources</u> were two letters he wrote and two transcripts of radio interviews he once gave.

principle—*n.* ideal; belief. A person who has <u>principles</u> is a person who does what she thinks is right, no matter what the consequences. Martin Luther King Jr. had <u>principles</u>. So did the activist Che Guevara.

production—*n.* the act of creating goods and services. Innovations in the <u>production</u> of Alpha-Bits caused the price of Alpha-Bits to fall. When they got cheaper, my mom started buying them again. That's when I started eating them again. I miss my expensive Fruity Pebbles!

profit—*n.* in business, the money left over after you subtract the costs of making something that you sell. If it costs a company $20 to make a CD player and they sell it for $50, their <u>profit</u> is $30.

prohibit—*v.* to not allow; to forbid. Laws are basically created to <u>prohibit</u> bad behavior like drunk driving and stealing.

prosecute—*v.* to bring a legal case against someone. Famous people are always getting <u>prosecuted</u> for breaking the law. Puff Daddy got <u>prosecuted</u> for carrying an illegal weapon and bribing people. Jennifer Lopez was with him when he got arrested, but she didn't get <u>prosecuted</u>. I wonder why? (Note: At press time, Mr. Daddy was wavering between the names Puff Daddy and P. Diddy. If he chose the latter, I apologize to Mr. Diddy for using his former name.)

prosperity—*n.* success and riches. America is known for being a land of <u>prosperity</u>—there are a lot of people in this country who are rich and middle class. Many countries have no <u>prosperity</u> at

Related Word
prosperous—**adj.
rich.**

Social Studies

- all—everyone is poor.

- **provoke**—*v.* to anger; to egg on. Many animals are quite peaceful until they are <u>provoked</u>. Most bears won't even pay you any attention, but if you <u>provoke</u> them by poking them with a stick or shooting at them, you are in big trouble.

- **radical**—*n.* someone who works for political or social revolution. Our country has a complicated relationship with <u>radicals</u>. When we were colonies breaking from England, we were the <u>radicals</u>, breaking the law. Now, as the most powerful nation in the world, we generally frown on <u>radicals</u>. And as a country based on the rule of law, revolution is not really our cup of tea. Just look at the famous <u>radicals</u> our country has had to see how complicated our relationship with them is.

- **ramification**—*n.* the by-product of an event or act. My sister Esther will be suffering several <u>ramifications</u> if she does not switch bedrooms with me, the first of which is: I will start calling her "Queen Doofus."

- **ratify**—*v.* to pass. After a law is written, it has to be <u>ratified</u> by both houses of Congress—the House of Representatives and the Senate, before it is signed (or vetoed) by the president.

- **ration**—*v.* to give out in restricted amounts, usually during wartime, to conserve resources. Food and fuel are often <u>rationed</u> during wartime so more resources can be devoted to fighting the battles.

- **rebellion**—*n.* a revolt against authority. Have you noticed how many words there are in this section that basically mean "revolt" and "rebel"? It is an important subject when it comes to the history of our country. <u>Rebellion</u> was involved when the colonies broke from England, and <u>rebels</u> have qualities that we as Americans value in a person. They do what they think is right, no matter what anyone thinks.

- **Reconstruction**—*proper noun.* the period after the Civil War when the South was controlled by the federal government, before those states were readmitted to the Union (1865-1877).

- **reform**—*v.* to change for the better. One of the great things about our government is that if a law—or the government—doesn't work, we can <u>reform</u> it by voting for representatives who want <u>reform</u>.

- **regulate**—*v.* to limit. The government <u>regulates</u> all kinds of things. The most important may be the toxic emissions from cars and power plants. The government <u>regulates</u> the poisons in those emissions by setting limits the companies must not exceed. If the company doesn't follow those <u>regulations</u>, the company gets fined.

Famous radicals include crazy writer Abbie Hoffman, presidential assassin Lee Harvey Oswald, and President Thomas Jefferson, who was a big fan of revolutions.

DOUBLE MEANING

ration—n. a quantity of food.

To remember Reconstruction, think of "reconstructing," or rebuilding, the country.

WhizQuiz

List three regulations at your school:
1. _____

2. _____

3. _____

repeal—*v.* to take back; to rescind. Sometimes a law is <u>repealed</u> because is was really a bad, bad idea. One of the reasons the colonies broke from England was that England wouldn't <u>repeal</u> tax laws that were really hard on the colonies.

representation—*n.* a person or persons who protect the rights and interests of a group. In the phrase "taxation without <u>representation</u>," it means not having <u>representatives</u> in the government looking out for your interests. The main reason the colonies broke with England was that they were being taxed, but had no say at all in how much they were taxed and why.

Representatives, House of—*proper noun.* one of two parts of the U.S. Congress. In the <u>House of Representatives,</u> states are proportionally represented: the greater the population of the state, the more representatives.

republic—*n.* a government where the people elect representatives to do their bidding. The United States is a <u>republic</u>.

reservation—*n.* land set aside by the government for a specific purpose (in this country, usually for housing the Native Americans that were driven from their land).

resolute—*adj.* firm; unwavering. I am <u>resolute</u> in my view that Limp Bizkit's music is just terrible, no matter how many records they sell.

restrain—*v.* to hold back. For example, I had to <u>restrain</u> my sister Esther when my friend Lamonte called her "Queen Doofus." She was quite angry. In American history, the New England <u>Restraining</u> Act was enacted by King Charles II in 1775. It <u>restrained</u> a handful of colonies from trading with anyone, and it made those colonies mad.

retaliation—*n.* the act of striking back after you get attacked. It is not good to start a fight, but sometimes you have to <u>retaliate</u> (see what my sister did in the definition above). Lincoln issued the Order of <u>Retaliation</u> in 1863 saying that if the South violated the rules of war by killing or enslaving captured Union soldiers, the Union would <u>retaliate </u>by doing the same to their soldiers.

Antonym
surrender—v.
to give up.

revenue—*n.* money made. Government gets its <u>revenue</u> from taxes. Companies get their <u>revenue</u> by selling things. I get my <u>revenue</u> from my allowance and mowing lawns.

secede—*v.* to break away from a unit. The South <u>seceded</u> from the United States in 1861. That's what started the Civil War, because President Lincoln would not let them do it without a fight. The South's <u>secession</u> was a pivotal moment in this country's history.

secondary source—*n.* a summary or an account of an event or person. When I wrote my report on Hall of Fame pitcher

Social Studies

Cy Young, the <u>secondary sources</u> I used included two *Sports Illustrated* articles on him and his biography posted on the website *majorleaguebaseball.com*.

sedition—*n.* words or deeds causing people to rebel against the state. During wartime, acts of <u>sedition</u> are not tolerated. In 1798, the U.S. Congress passed the Alien and <u>Sedition</u> Acts to prevent political dissidents and the press from interfering with preparations for war with France.

Anto**nym**

integration—n. the
combination of
groups of people.

segregation—*n.* the separation of people who are different. Blacks were <u>segregated</u> from white society for years in this country. In some churches, women and men are <u>segregated</u>, with women sitting on one side, men on the other. Boys are often <u>segregated</u> from girls in gym class. <u>Segregation</u> keeps people apart.

Senate—*proper noun* one of two parts of the U.S. Congress. *Note*: Each state, regardless of its size, is represented by two senators in the <u>Senate</u>.

sovereign—*n.* a king or queen. We don't have any sovereigns in our country. England still has its <u>sovereigns</u>, but they don't have any power anymore. They are just symbols of England's past.

WhizTip

To remember
subversive means
"undermining,"
remember sub
means "under."

subversive—*adj.* undermining. As part of preparing for a war against France, Thomas Jefferson signed the Alien and Sedition Acts which outlawed <u>subversive</u> behavior, like criticizing the government. Now we can criticize the government as much as we want.

succession—*n.* the process of following in order. There has been a <u>succession</u> of kings and queens in the history of most European nations. Sometimes the <u>succession</u> went smoothly. Sometimes, it was bloody.

WhizTip

To remember
suffrage,
remember
people "suffer"
when they don't
have the right
to vote.

suffrage—*n.* the right to vote. Women gained <u>suffrage</u> in this country in 1920. Eighteen-year-olds gained <u>suffrage</u> after the Vietnam War when they argued that if they could go to war, why couldn't they vote?

surplus—*n.* left-overs. You have probably heard of the federal government's budget <u>surplus</u>. That's the money left over after the government uses the taxes we pay to pay its bills.

sympathizer—*n.* someone who agrees with something and wants to help; someone who is <u>sympathetic</u> to a person or cause. In American history, the word is used in the term "communist <u>sympathizers</u>," which refers to people who agreed with the communists and helped them out in the early twentieth century.

Taoism—*proper noun.* a religion based on the teachings of Chinese philosopher Lao-tse. One of its main teachings is that you should be like water, flowing through and around your problems instead of butting up against them.

tariff—*n.* tax on imports and exports. High <u>tariffs</u> on the colonies' imports and exports made colonists' mad at England. You know what happened next.

tax—*n.* a payment made by individuals and businesses to the government; an extra fee put on goods and services.

temperance—*n.* the act of not drinking alcohol. There was a <u>temperance</u> movement in the United States in the early twentieth century that made drinking alcohol illegal. That was when gangsters like Al Capone made millions selling illegal booze.

textile—*n.* cloth. Massachusetts is a big producer of <u>textiles</u>.

topography—*n.* the physical aspects of a place or region. You've probably seen a <u>topographical</u> map—a map that shows a region's physical landscape instead of roads and landmarks.

totalitarianism—*n.* a type of government in which one person or party has absolute control. See my definition for *despotism* for more information (they're pretty much the same thing).

transcend—*v.* to surpass; to overcome. Sometimes you have to <u>transcend</u> your limitations to reach your goals. If your vocabulary is a limitation for you, this book should help you <u>transcend</u> that obstacle.

Treasury—*proper noun.* the part of the government in charge of the money supply. Our <u>Treasury</u> Department makes sure there is enough, but not too much, money floating around to keep the economy moving.

tyranny—*n.* total power used in a cruel way. Once I accused the judges at skateboarding regionals of practicing <u>tyranny</u>. I thought they were giving me low marks on a whim, just because they could, because they had all the power.

unanimous—*adj.* being in complete agreement. In a <u>unanimous</u> decision, everyone votes the same way. 100 percent of the people vote the same way. When we took a vote from the students at school about our dress code, the students voted <u>unanimously</u> to repeal it.

urban—*adj.* related to the city. Lots of big cities around the country have been undergoing <u>urban</u> renewal, which means they are working to improve the quality of their inner cities and downtown areas.

utopia—*n.* a perfect world. Many systems of government promise their followers a <u>utopia</u> on Earth. I think Hawaii is the closest anyone has come to <u>utopia</u> yet!

verdict—*n.* a decision in a court case. It is the job of a jury to reach a <u>verdict</u> in a case. When members of a jury don't reach a <u>verdict</u>, it's called a "hung jury."

Whiz Quiz

Name a limitation you have had to transcend in your life:

_____
_____
_____

Related Word

majority—**adj. In a majority vote, more than 50 percent of the people vote one way, but not everybody.**

Antonym

rural—**adj. related to the countryside.**

veteran—*n.* someone who has fought in a war. We celebrate Veterans Day to remember the people who fought our wars. My great-grandfather is a veteran—he fought in World War II.

veto—*n.* rejection of a proposal. In our government, a veto is a president's vote against legislation passed by Congress. Presidents often veto legislation they don't agree with.

Whig—*proper noun.* an eighteenth- and nineteenth-century political party in England opposed to the Tories; a nineteenth-century party in America opposed to the Democrats. The Tories and the Democrats are still around. The Whigs aren't. Poor Whigs. Maybe their weird name did them in. Could you vote for a Whig?

WhizWords

communism
democracy
despotism
fascism
federalism
imperialism
republic
totalitarianism

Social Studies

Government

I was over at my great-grandfather's assisted-living complex the other day, and he was going on and on about World War II. He's a good guy, but when you get him started on World War II, you might as well pull up a chair because you're going to be there for a while. Anyway, he was talking about **fascism** and **communism** and all of these different kinds of governments I have only heard of in history class.

It made me realize that I wrongly assumed that all countries are **democracies** like ours. When my great-grandfather was growing up, Germany had a **fascist** government, Russia was part of the Soviet Union and was a **communist** country, **imperialism** was the favorite kind of government for all kinds of kings in the Middle East, and the African countries that weren't run as colonies by France and England were run by **despots.**

My great grandfather lived in crazy times! Today, the Middle East oil countries are still pretty much all run by kings, and Africa is still a hotbed of **despotism**, but lots of the rest of the countries—like Germany and Japan— have gone **democratic.**

Related Word

nationalism—n. Nationalism is a bad thing when it means you really like your country, but hate all the other countries. Nazi Germany was based on intense nationalism. The Nazis were going to rule the whole world, and kill anyone they thought was unworthy of being a member of the Third Reich.

IDENTIFY THE GOVERNMENT TYPE

Following are some countries that have gone through some big changes over the years. If you don't know what kind of government was in place on the dates I give you (and from the hints in my descriptions), do some research in the library or on the Internet to find out. You will be very surprised by what you find.

Country	Year	Hint
England	1714	King George I assumes the throne.
Texas	1836	Texas is an independent republic.
United States	1897	William McKinley is elected our 25th president.
Germany	1935	Hitler rules with an iron fist.
Jordan	1953	King Hussein assumes his hereditary position.
Cambodia	1976	The totalitarian Khmer Rouge wreak havoc.
England	1979	Margaret Thatcher is elected the first woman prime minister.

Whenever you hear about a country in the news that you don't know anything about, do some research and figure out what kind of government it has. I've been doing this for the last few months whenever I hear about a country in Africa or Asia, because I don't know very much about those two continents. It is really scary how few democracies there are out there!

Exercises

acculturation
colonize
diffuse
genocide
indigenous
inhabitant
migration

Social Studies

Culture Clash

Related Word

manifest destiny—n.
The United States used manifest destiny **as its justification for destroying the** indigenous **cultures of North America and committing** genocide **against this continent's native population.**

A culture is like a situation comedy. It starts out one day with an **indigenous** cast—its original actors. As the **inhabitants** get to know each other, they form relationships, customs and a special language. On a sitcom, the language consists of catch phrases, like "What you talkin bout Willis?" (from *Diff'rent Strokes*) and "yadda yadda yadda" (from *Seinfeld*).

After a few seasons, things usually get a little boring, so a new character or two are introduced to the sitcom's culture. Sometimes they **migrate** from another popular sitcom, hoping that some of their fans from that show will start to watch their new show. The new cast members quickly become **acculturated**, learning the customs and language of their new show.

If the show is popular enough and lasts long enough, some of the cast members may leave and star in their own spin-offs (like *Angel* spinning off from *Buffy the Vampire Slayer*), thereby **colonizing** another night of the network's prime-time lineup. As long as the ratings stay high, everyone is happy, and the shows live on. But when the ratings dip for a period of time, there is only one fate for a sitcom culture: **genocide**. The show is killed off.

The actors that do survive usually wander around for a while, getting a few small parts in bad movies and doing some commercials, before they **diffuse** across the sitcom landscape, starring as different characters in different shows, becoming **acculturated** to newer, more powerful sitcoms.

CULTURE CLASH ANALOGIES

That was really fun to write. So for this exercise, I want you to use my little story as a model and think of another analogy for how cultures clash, mingle, and mix with one another. I used the rough and tumble world of television sitcoms. Here are a few topics you can use to write a short essay about cultures clashing:

Pro sports teams	**Neighboring schools**
Pop music groups	**Neighboring states**
Toy companies	**Political parties**

You don't have to use these suggestions, just make sure you use all of the "Culture Clash" words in your analogy. When you are done, check the words against the definitions and see if you used them correctly.

WhizWords

abolitionist
bias
discriminate
emancipation
feminism
integration
intolerant
oppress
persecute
segregation
suffrage

Social Studies

Inequality

People rebel because they feel they are being **oppressed** or **discriminated** against. **Feminists** fight for the rights of women every day because women don't have the same rights as men. **Abolitionists** fought for the freedom of slaves, who didn't have any rights at all. In fact, the history of our country is filled with situations where individuals had to overcome **bias**. It was once common to **discriminate** based on race and gender. And our country is called the land of the free! So you can just imagine what life is like in countries where equality isn't even talked about, much less strived for.

Luckily in the United States, we have made great strides. There is pretty much universal **suffrage** now—everyone over the age of eighteen can vote. Our public schools, public places, and the military are all **integrated**, too. **Segregation** used to keep white people and black people apart.

Even so, there is still a lot of **intolerance** around. Lots of the advances in equality have happened in the past twenty or thirty years, but old habits die hard. So some people still use stereotypes to judge those who are different than they are.

Related Word

diversity—**n.**
variety.
Diversity **and**
integration **can**
help people
learn that
stereotypes
and biases
are shallow
and stupid.

SUFFRAGE FOR FASHION MODELS

The fight for equal rights is a serious business. People have given their lives so that others might have equal opportunity. However, for this exercise, let's lighten things up a little. Pretend there is only one group left in this country that is being discriminated against: skinny fashion models. Now, get a pencil and paper and write a make-believe history about how skinny fashion models go from being segregated, discriminated against, and not having the right to vote, to being integrated, having equal rights, and having suffrage in the year 2050. Use as many of the words above as you can. You can start your essay right here if you'd like.

ESSAY

The History of Skinny Fashion Models' Fight
For Suffrage in the Twenty-First Century

_____

_____

_____

_____

_____

_____

_____

_____

WhizWords

carpetbagger
debate
impeachment
inaugurate
lame duck
mandate
opposition
partisan
populism
reform

The best way to build your vocabulary is to read, read, and read some more. Newspapers are a good source of reading material. You'll find new information about things you're interested in every day.

Social Studies

Politics

Did you pay attention to the 2000 presidential race? When it started I didn't pay too much attention. But my dad is such a big Gore fan, he made me go to some rallies, and I started to get excited. And then the election! Nobody won! It took them about a month to figure out who the next president was going to be. It was the first time I stopped thinking about baseball and started thinking about something else outside of school.

The election got me started reading the political stories in the newspaper. That's when I started to realize there were a ton of words I didn't know very well. For example—**carpetbagger.** Have you ever heard that word? And **lame duck.** I mean, what do ducks have to do with politics, especially ducks that waddle with a limp?

Apparently a lot, because **lame duck** and **carpetbagger** kept coming up over and over again, along with **impeachment, mandate,** and **partisan.** It's no wonder they are important to know for social studies tests. If you know these words, you will be a more informed citizen, and, therefore, probably vote for the right person more often. (At least that's the idea.)

READ THE POLITICS PAGE

Keep this book handy. Pick up the latest copy of your local newspaper. Not the free handout you get at the grocery store with all of the used cars for sale—the real thing. Start with the Sunday paper if you can—it's usually about twice as thick. Now find the stories about local and national politics and start reading. Whenever you see one of the WhizWords above, underline it. Write down the number of times each word appears.

Keep doing this for one week. That's right—read the political stories every day for one week. People may think you are crazy, but do it anyway. You can still read the sports page and the comics (my personal favorites), but read political news first. Underline, count, write the "Politics" words listed above in this chart

	Day 1	Day 2	Day 3	Day 4	Day 5	Day 6	Day 7
carpetbagger							
debate							
impeachment							
inaugurate							
lame duck							
mandate							
opposition							
partisan							
populism							
reform							

Which word won? Which came in second? Make sure you know the Top Three like the back of your hand, and make sure you know the rest of 'em like the front of your hand.

Social Studies

Economics

Did I say this country was all about freedom and equality? Just ask Alex Rodriguez, who signed a ten-year contract with the Texas Rangers for almost $250 million, what this country is all about. Show me the money!

I mean, I love Alex Rodriguez. He is definitely the best shortstop in the American League. But $250 million? I think he gets like $50,000 for each at bat or something like that. I only get $10 a week for my allowance! Maybe A-Rod can spare a few hundred bucks?

No wonder tests ask so many questions about the U.S. **economy** and our **free enterprise** system. As a citizen of the richest country on the planet, it is important that you know how **capitalism** works so you can carry on the tradition. Especially if you end up being a major league shortstop.

READ THE BUSINESS PAGE

This exercise is basically a repeat of the "Politics" exercise. After you get done with your week of reading the political stories in the paper, I want you to do a week of reading the business stories in the paper. I know—and you thought it couldn't get any more boring than politics!

Here's your chart for the week:

	Day 1	Day 2	Day 3	Day 4	Day 5	Day 6	Day 7
boom and bust economy							
capital							
capitalism							
commerce							
commodity							
consumption							
currency							
distribution							
economy							
entrepreneur							
free enterprise							
production							
profit							
tax							

Again, know the Top Three like the back of your hand and the rest like the front of your hand.

Chapter 3

Math

angle—*n.* the figure formed when two lines meet at a point. There are three kinds of <u>angles</u>: *acute* (less than 90°), *obtuse* (greater than 90°), and *right* (90°).

acute angle   obtuse angle   right angle

angle—*n.* oh yeah, there are two more kinds of angles—complementary and supplementary. <u>Complementary angles</u> add up to 90°. <u>Supplementary angles</u> add up to 180°.

area—*n.* the amount of surface on a figure. For example, a rectangle's <u>area</u> is length x width. A triangle's <u>area</u> is 1/2 base x height. A circle's <u>area</u> is πr^2. Just remember: <u>area</u> is the amount of space inside the lines.

associative—*adj.* the property that allows two or more real numbers to be added or multiplied, regardless of their grouping, without changing the result. *Example*: Addition and multiplication are both <u>associative</u>.

average—*n.* what you get when you add up a bunch of numbers and then divide by the number of numbers you added up. The <u>average</u> of the numbers 9, 13, 28, 72, 83 = (9 + 13 + 28 + 72 + 83) ÷ 5 = 205 ÷ 5 = 41. So 41 is the <u>average</u> of those five numbers.

axes—*n.* the plural form of axis. <u>Axes</u> are the horizontal and vertical lines that make up a graph. They are usually (but not always) named the *x*-axis and *y*-axis.

bisect—*v.* to divide into two usually equal parts. In math, a line or a point usually <u>bisects</u> another line. It cuts that line in two. Once in science we had to dissect a frog, and I had to <u>bisect</u> its brain—I actually cut its brain in half. I almost fainted.

capacity—*n.* the amount something can hold. *Example*: My dad's Honda's gas tank has a <u>capacity</u> of 12 gallons of gas.

chord—*n.* a line segment joining two points on a curve.

circumference—*n.* the length of the boundary of a circle. If you took a circle and straightened out the line that surrounds it and measured it, that would be the <u>circumference</u>. The formula to find a circle's

46

circumference is $2\pi r$, with r standing for *radius*.

commission—*n.* a percentage fee that a salesperson gets for making a sale. On tests, sometimes you have to calculate the dollar value of a certain percent <u>commission</u>. So if a salesperson gets a 10% <u>commission</u> for selling a $590 computer, she makes $59.

common factor—*n.* a factor that divides evenly into two or more different numbers. *Example:* The greatest <u>common factor</u> of 10 and 15 is 5.

common multiple—*n.* a multiple shared by two or more different numbers. *Example:* The least <u>common multiple</u> of 10 and 15 is 30.

commutative—*adj.* the property that allows two or more numbers to be added or multiplied in any order without changing the result. *Example*:

$$a + b = b + a \qquad a \times b = b \times a$$

composite—*n.* a number that is able to be factored by numbers other than itself and 1. Just remember that any <u>composite</u> MUST be factorable and prime numbers are NOT <u>composites</u>.

congruent—*adj.* having the same shape and size. If you put one <u>congruent</u> shape on top of another, they would be exactly the same. In math, the word is often used to describe <u>congruent</u> triangles.

consecutive—*adj.* occurring in order, one right after the other. In math, it is used to describe <u>consecutive</u> numbers in a number pattern. Players also talk about how hard it is to play on <u>consecutive</u> days in sports like baseball and basketball because they don't get to rest between games.

converge—*v.* to come together at a point. Lines <u>converge</u>. So do rivers. In Pennsylvania, the Allegheny and Monongahela rivers <u>converge</u> to form the Ohio River.

convert—*v.* to change from one system of measurement to another. Most often used when <u>converting</u> our system of measurements to the metric system. See the <u>conversions</u> page at the end of this section for some common measurements and <u>conversions</u>.

coordinates—*n.* a set of two numbers that shows where a point goes on a <u>coordinate</u> plane.

Whiz Tip

To remember composite, **think of the word "component."** A composite **number has "component" factors.**

Whiz Quiz

Pick the next number in these number patterns:

3, 6, 9, 12, __
–3, –1, 1, 3, __
3/4, 1 1/2, 2 1/4, __

DOUBLE MEANING
convert—v.
To change from one or set of beliefs to another (social studies).

47

Math

$$\frac{3}{5} \longleftarrow \text{denominator}$$

Bar Graph

**Circle Graph
(Pie Graph)**

coordinate plane—*n.* a plane on which *x* and *y* axes have been added so one can plot coordinates on it.

data—*n.* facts and figures; the information you are given in a math problem. Test questions are always asking you to look at the <u>data</u> and answer the question.

denominator—*n.* the number under the line in a fraction.

diagonal—*n.* in a polygon, a line slanting from one corner to the other. The "Diver Down" flag used by scuba divers has a <u>diagonal</u> line across it—that's a good way to get a visual of the word <u>diagonal</u>.

diameter—*n.* the length across the middle of a circle. If you are given the radius of the circle, double it to get the diameter: $d = 2r$.

distributive—*adj.* the <u>distributive</u> property is an algebra property that helps you multiply a single term and two or more terms inside parentheses, when the terms inside the parentheses are like terms. *Example*:

$$3(4+5) = 3(4) + 3(5) = 27$$

divisor—*n.* the number that divides another number (the dividend).

domain—*n.* the set of the first coordinates of a group of ordered pairs. (The set of second coordinates is the *range*.) In the set of coordinates $\{(5,12), (6,18), \text{and } (7,20)\}$, the <u>domain</u> is $\{5,6,7\}$.

edge—*n.* where two surfaces of a solid intersect.

exponent—*n.* a number off to the upper right of another number that shows the power to which the number is raised. That means whatever the <u>exponent</u> is, you multiply a number times itself that many times. *Example:* $4^3 = 4 \times 4 \times 4 = 64$.

face—*n.* the flat side of a solid figure.

factor—*n.* a number that can be multiplied with others to achieve a product. Hmm. How can I put this? Pick a number. The numbers you multiply to get that number are its <u>factors</u>. Take the number 27, for instance. Some of its <u>factors</u> are $3 \times 3 \times 3$ (= 27). Some others are 9×3 (= 27). Some others are 27×1 (= 27). The number 13 has <u>factors</u> of 13×1 (= 13). Note: 13 is also a prime number—which means its only <u>factors</u> are itself and 1.

graph—*n.* a diagram. You need to know how to read two main kinds of graphs—<u>circle graphs</u> and <u>bar graphs</u>. A <u>circle graph</u> is also called a <u>pie graph</u>. The different sized slices of pie show relative proportions of something, like the amount of attention four brothers and sisters get from their parents. A <u>bar graph</u> measures things on an *x* and *y* axis. The *x* axis stands for one thing (like years) and the *y* axis stands for another (like height). *Note:* You may also see <u>line graphs</u> here and there: they look like a jagged mountain top set on an *x* axis.

hexagon—*n.* a polygon with six sides.

histogram *n.*—a special type of bar graph where the width of the bars can be different.

horizontal—*adj.* straight across. To remember the word, think of a "horizon."

hypotenuse—*n.* the longest side of a right triangle; the side opposite the 90⁰ angle. About the only time you will see questions about the <u>hypotenuse</u> is in questions about right triangles.

integer—*n.* positive whole numbers, negative whole numbers, and zero. No fractions and no decimals are <u>integers</u>—ever! Think of <u>integers</u> as having too much "integrity" to get involved with messy fractions and decimals.

integral—*adj.* in math, it means a number expressable as an integer or a group of integers.

intercept—*n.* the place where a line, curve, or surface crosses the axis on a graph.

interest—*n.* a charge for a loan, usually expressed as a percentage of that loan. Sometimes a math problem will ask you to figure out how much total <u>interest</u> will be charged over the course of a loan.

interpret—*v.* to form a conclusion from a group of data. I <u>interpreted</u> 100 years of hitting statistics and came up with this: players today are better hitters.

intersect—*v.* to cross each other. Lines <u>intersect</u> on graphs. To remember the word, think of street <u>intersections</u>—where streets cross each other.

inverse—*n.* the reciprocal of a quantity. The <u>inverse</u> of 2/3 is 3/2.

irrational number—*n.* a number that cannot be expressed as a fraction or decimal. Like π. You can put an <u>irrational number</u> on a number line, but you can't express the number precisely, like you can with 1.5 and –3. (See the definition for *rational number* if it's still confusing.)

line segment—*n.* a portion of a line bounded by two points.

mean—*n.* see the definition for *average*; they are the same thing.

median—*n.* in a group of numbers, it is the one in the middle or the average of the two numbers in the middle. *Example*: Here is a group of numbers: 23, 31, 67, 78, 86, 165, 254. The <u>median</u> is 78—it is the middle number in this series.

mixed number—*n.* a number made up of a whole number and a fraction. *Example:* 6 7/8.

mode—*n.* in a group of numbers, it is the number that occurs most often. *Example*: Here is a group of numbers: 23, 24, 24, 25, 26, 27, 28, 29, 29, 30, 31, 32, 32, 32, 33, 34. The <u>mode</u> is 32. It occurs three times—the most of any number in this series.

negative number—*n.* a number less than zero, indicated by a minus sign (–). On a number line, the numbers to the left of 0 are <u>negative numbers</u>.

net—*n.* 1) a thing you catch butterflies with. 2) a connected set of polygons in a single plane that can be folded to form a polyhedron. For example, if you carefully peel back the glued panels of a cereal

WhizTip

To remember median, think of the median that separates one side of a highway from the other. It runs down the middle of the highway.

$$\frac{3}{5}$$

numerator

box, the opened, flattened box is the <u>net</u>.

numerator—*n.* the number on top of the line in a fraction; the number that is divided by the denominator.

order of operations—*n.* the sequence by which you do the operations in an equation. To remember the correct <u>order of operations</u>, think of PEMDAS ("Please Excuse My Dear Aunt Sally"). The <u>order of operations</u> is: parentheses, exponents, multiplication and division, and then addition and subtraction.

parallel—*adj.* relating to lines traveling alongside each other at the same distance without ever touching. Train tracks are <u>parallel</u>.

parallelogram—*n.* a four-sided figure with parallel opposite sides.

pentagon—*n.* a five-sided figure.

perimeter—*n.* the outside edge of an object or shape. Think about soldiers patrolling the <u>perimeter</u> of their outpost. That means they are patrolling the edges of their camp, making sure the enemy isn't planning any funny business.

perpendicular—*adj.* relating to lines meeting each other at a right (90⁰) angle. <u>Perpendicular</u> is kind of the opposite of *parallel*. They are mentioned in the same sentence—and the same math problem—all the time.

perspective

perspective—*n.* the appearance of depth or three dimensions. Think about drawing a road that recedes into the distance— the sides of the road get closer together as they go away into the distance. Oh heck, sometimes a picture is worth a thousand words, so just look at the picture of the road on the left. That's <u>perspective</u>.

place value—*n.* the position of a numeral in a number. *Example:* In the number 6,789, the <u>place value</u> of 6 is "thousands," the <u>place value</u> of 7 is "hundreds," the <u>place value</u> of 8 is "tens," and the <u>place value</u> of 9 is "ones."

plane—*n.* a flat surface. *Note:* Think of "the Great *Plains*."

polygon—*n.* a flat shape with three or more straight sides. A <u>polygon</u> is any shape with flat sides, really, from a triangle to a rectangle to an octagon to whatever a shape with 28 sides is called, and beyond . . . .

positive number—*n.* a number greater than zero. On a number line, the numbers to the right of 0 are <u>positive numbers</u>.

power—*n.* an exponent. *Example:* 67 to the <u>power</u> of 12 = 67^{12}.

prime number—*n.* a positive, whole number with only itself and 1 as factors. That means you can't divide any other number into it without getting a remainder. 17 is a <u>prime number</u>. 23 is a <u>prime number</u>. Try all night, you can't divide any other numbers into them without getting a remainder. (See the definition for *factor* for more information.)

probability—*n.* the chance that something will happen. *Example:* If you flip a coin, the <u>probability</u> that it will turn up

On the Test
What is the probability that dinner consisted of a hot dog, orange juice, and cake?

heads is 1/2, or 50%, since there are two possible outcomes.

product—*n.* the answer to a multiplication problem. The product of 3 x 6 is 18.

project—*v.* to predict logically how something will play out in the future. *Example:* At my current rate of consumption, I project that by 2020, I will have eaten 8,236 Drake's Cakes.

proportion—*n.* a comparison of equivalent ratios. *Example*: 3/6 = 1/2, also written 3:6 = 1:2.

Pythagorean theorem—*n.* for right triangles, the sum of the squares of a right triangle's sides is equal to the square of the hypotenuse. $a^2 + b^2 = hyp^2$. (See the definitions for *hypotenuse* and *triangles* for more information.)

quadrant—*n.* 1) one-fourth of the circumference of a circle. 2) one of the four sections of a coordinate plane.

quadrilateral—*n.* a four-sided polygon. Squares, rectangles, and rhombuses are all quadrilaterals.

radius—*n.* the line from the center of a circle to its outside edge. The radius is half a circle's diameter.

random—*adj.* having no pattern or reason; out of the blue. Lottery numbers are picked at random.

range—*n.* the difference between the highest and lowest numbers in a group of numbers.

rate—*n.* one thing measured in terms of another thing. Miles per hour. Words per minute. Gallons per flush. Inches per year. Those are all rates.

ratio—*n.* the relationship between two quantities. Ratios aren't always expressed as fractions. The ratio of 4 to 9 can be written as 4/9 or 4:9; the ratio of 6 to 7 can be written as 6/7 or 6:7.

rational number—*n.* a number that can be expressed as a ratio of two integers. 7 is a rational number because it can be expressed as 7/1. –2/3 is a rational number. 45.4 is a rational number.

reciprocal—*n.* the quotient of a quantity divided into 1. *Example*: The reciprocal of 1/7 is 7/1. The reciprocal of 6/7 is 7/6.

reflection—*n.* a shape that is flipped, so it's the same, but backwards. Think of it like your reflection in the mirror. All the sides are the same length and the angles are the same size; they are just positioned exactly opposite of where they were.

rhombus—*n.* a polygon with four equal sides (but not necessarily four equal angles); an equilateral parallelogram.

rotation—*n.* movement in a circular motion around a fixed point. When a geometric shape is rotated, its shape stays the same but the side that was on the bottom may now be on the top.

scale—*n.* when talking about models, scale is the relationship between the size of the model and the size of the real-life object. So if a scale model of an airplane is 1:8, that means the real airplane is eight times as big as the model.

On the Test
How would the product **5 x 5 x 5** be expressed in exponential notation?

Related Word
random sample—**n. a group of numbers or values chosen out of the blue.**

DOUBLE MEANING
rate—**v. to judge; to rank (social studies).**

On the Test
A scale model of the ship is 1/12 the ship's actual size. Which proportion should be used to measure its length?

scatterplot—*n.* a graph used to show the relationship between two or more variables. So if one class's math scores were on a <u>scatterplot</u>, and lots of students were getting Bs, it would look like this:

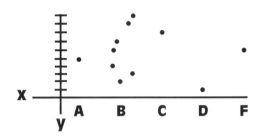

scientific notation—*n.* a way of writing numbers in terms of powers of ten. For example, 3,414 is 3.414×10^3.

simplify—*v.* 1) to turn a fraction into an integer, mixed number, or base fraction. *Examples:* $42/6 = 7$; $9/18 = 1/2$. 2) to combine expressions that have the same variables in an equation.

slope—*n.* the measure of the steepness of a line. The equation for the <u>slope</u> of a line is rise/run (vertical change/horizontal change).

square root—*n.* the divisor of a number that when multiplied by itself gives that number. So 6 is the <u>square root</u> of 36 because 6^2 is 36. The symbol for <u>square root</u> is $\sqrt{\ }$, so the <u>square root</u> of 36 can be written as $\sqrt{36}$.

stem-and-leaf plot—*n.* a way to organize groups of data, where the "tens" digits are called the <u>stems</u> and the "ones" digits are called the <u>leaves</u>.

surface—*n.* the boundary of a three-dimensional shape.

Symmetry

symbol—*n.* something that stands for something else.

symmetry—*n.* a balanced arrangement; the stuff on one side of a dividing line matches the stuff on the other. If you draw a line down the middle of your face, the parts on the left match the parts on the right. Your face has <u>symmetry</u>. It is <u>symmetrical</u>. So are some shapes and some graphs.

three-dimensional—*adj.* having three dimensions: height, width, and depth. Any real object is <u>three-dimensional</u>. Also written as <u>3-D</u>.

translation—*n.* the movement of a geometric figure without turning or flipping it (also called *slide*).

transversal—*n.* a line that intersects a group of lines.

trapezoid—*n.* a quadrilateral with two parallel sides.

trial and error—*n.* a method of solving a problem by trying several guesses and eliminating those that turn out to be wrong. Scientific experiments often involve <u>trial and error</u>, and you can use the system to tackle a tough math problem, too. If you can't solve a math problem the right way, there is always <u>trial and error</u>.

triangle—*n.* shape with three sides and three angles. There are four kinds of <u>triangles</u> you need to know:

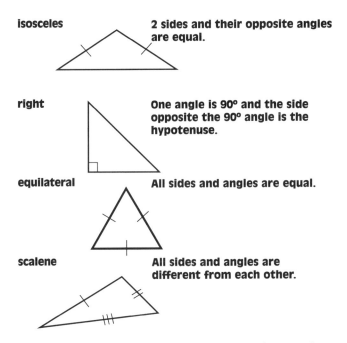

isosceles — 2 sides and their opposite angles are equal.

right — One angle is 90° and the side opposite the 90° angle is the **hypotenuse**.

equilateral — All sides and angles are equal.

scalene — All sides and angles are different from each other.

two-dimensional—*adj.* on a single plane; having no volume.

value—*n.* in math, an assigned number or numerical quantity.

variable—*n.* a symbol whose value can change. In math, the <u>variable</u> is usually called *x* or *y*. That means you can plug in different numbers for the <u>variable</u> *x* or *y* or *z* or whatever. To remember the word, think of watching a weather report. The weatherman often says that "winds are <u>variable</u>," and weather itself is always <u>variable</u> (changing).

Venn diagram—*n.* a diagram that uses circles to represent relationships among groups.

vertical—*adj.* going straight up and down. Like a flag pole.

volume—*n.* the amount of space something occupies. You can get Coca-Cola in all kinds of different <u>volumes</u>, from a 12-ounce can to a 16-ounce bottle to a 3-liter bottle. I prefer the 3-liter bottle.

whole number—*n.* an integer. Positive or negative. Not a fraction, not a decimal, not an irrational number. Just nice, clean integers are <u>whole numbers</u>.

Whiz Quiz

Solve the following problems with the variables $x=2$ and $y=3$

$2x$
$4y$
$x - y$
$2y + 7x$
$-2x - 4y$

Math
Measurements Page

METRIC AND
BRITISH IMPERIAL MEASUREMENTS

Measurement conversion charts are provided on most math tests, so it's important you know how to read them. Measuring is the only time I wish I was European. They have things so easy when it comes to measuring. As you probably know, their metric system is all based on tens. Anyway, here are the measurements that are used most often on tests—in metric and British Imperial (that's what we use). Don't ask me why we use British Imperial and the English use metrics. Because I don't know.

BRITISH IMPERIAL
Distance

Foot	12 inches
Yard	3 feet
Mile	1,760 yards

Volume

Pint	16 ounces
Quart	2 pints
Gallon	4 quarts

Weight

Pound	16 ounces
Ton	2,000 pounds

METRIC
Distance

Centimeter	10 millimeters
Meter	100 centimeters
Kilometer	1,000 meters

Volume

Liter	1,000 milliliters

Weight

Gram	1,000 milligrams
Kilogram	1,000 grams
Metric ton	1,000 kilograms

COMMON CONVERSIONS
(ALL CONVERSIONS ARE APPROXIMATE)
Distance

BRITISH IMPERIAL	METRIC
Inch	about 3 centimeters
Yard	about 1 meter
Mile	about 1.6 kilometers

Volume

BRITISH IMPERIAL	METRIC
Ounce	about 29 milliliters
Cup	about 1/4 liter
Gallon	about 3.79 liters

Weight

BRITISH IMPERIAL	METRIC
Ounce	about 29 grams
Pound	about 450 grams (about 1/2 kilogram)

WhizWords

bar graph*
circle graph*
coordinates
line graph*

*See definition
for <u>graph</u>.

Math

Graphs

So many people say—Why do I need to learn all this math? I'll never use it in real life. I think I'll spend my time shopping on eBay.

Well, nothing could be further from the truth. Lots of people use math every day. In baseball, they use math to calculate hitters' batting averages. Players can then use those batting averages to negotiate their salaries. Then, when they are buying their yachts and mansions, they use math to calculate sales tax and change. Even if you're not an All-Star baseball player, you'll still need to know math. How else are you going to budget to save up for those great deals on eBay?

Now that you are convinced, let's start with something relatively simple that is used all the time: a graph. There is nothing better for explaining things in an easy-to-read format than a chart or a graph

USING MATH TO EXPLAIN YOUR LIFE
You can use a graph to represent just about any relationship. I have created the following graphs to represent:

My test grades last grading period:
67, 92, 89, 94, 78, 81, 88, 97

The four TV shows I watch the most, in relative proportion to the amount of time spent viewing:

Digimon 10%
Moesha 30%
Buffy 20%
Baseball 40%

My height over the years:

Years	3	6	9	12
Feet	3	3.5	4	4.75

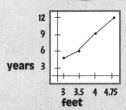

Now you draw the same three graphs for your most recent math grades, viewing time for your favorite TV shows, and your height at different ages. Try to think of three more things you can represent on a graph. Here are some ideas: raises or drops in your allowance in the last two years, the proportions of kinds of food you eat every day, and the amount of time you spend daily on various activities like sleeping, eating, going to school, doing homework, e-mailing your friends, and so on.

WhizWords

integer
irrational number
mixed number
negative number
positive number
prime number
rational number
whole number

Math

Number Types

Still not convinced of math's importance in your everyday existence? I was like you once, before I saw the light. One part of math you can't dispute is that numbers are everywhere. We measure ingredients, tell time, and count the days until summer vacation.

What you probably don't do while you are counting the days to summer vacation is think about what kind of number you have in your head. The "31" in "31 days until summer vacation" is an **integer**, a **positive number**, a **prime number**, a **rational number**, and a **whole number**. Those are the kinds of things you need to know for all kinds of tests. So let's review.

NUMBERS YOU SEE EVERY DAY

Label each of the numbers with all of the number types from above that match. If none match, write "none." I'll do the first couple so you get the idea.

17 years old   integer, positive number, prime number, rational number, whole number

–3 degrees   integer, negative number, rational number, whole number

$.79 Snickers bar

.327 batting average

2 1/2 weeks

4 hours

–12 under par

a drink coaster with a circumference of 6π (okay, I'm stretching here)

WhizWords

average
mean
median
mode

Math
Number Relationships

Whether you believe that math affects your everyday life or not, you still have to take tests about it. One thing that shows up on all sorts of math tests is number relationships. Questions about number relationships usually involve long lists of numbers and ask you to figure out the **mean**, **median**, or **mode**. Sometimes all three.

Just remember:

- **mean** (means **average**)
- **median** (in the middle of the road)
- **mode** (sounds like most)

So let's get to it.

MORE NUMBERS YOU SEE EVERY DAY

Find the mean, median, and mode of my grades last year on tests in English language arts, math, science, and social studies.

		Mean	Median	Mode
English	56, 92, 87, 79, 95, 92, 99			
Math	78, 82, 91, 79, 78, 97, 93			
Science	94, 91, 99, 100, 89, 94, 94			
Social Studies	102, 84, 72, 67, 84, 94, 84			

Find the *mean, median,* and *mode* of these three baseball players' batting averages over their careers.

		Mean	Median	Mode
Paul O'Neill	.333, .256, .252, .276, .270, .256, .246, .311, .359, .300, .302, .324, .317, .285, .283			
Manny Ramirez	.269, .308, .309, .328, .294, .333, .351			
Alex Rodriguez	.232, .358, .300, .310, .285, .316			
Nomar Garciaparra	.241, .306, .328, .357, .372			
Tony Gwynn	.289, .309, .351, .317, .329, .370, .313, .336, .309, .317, .317, .358, .394, .368, .353, .372, .321, .338, .323			

WhizTip

For more practice, line up your grades from last semester or last year and find the mean, median, and mode.

Chapter 4

Science

- **absorb**—*v.* to soak up. Commercials for paper towels brag about how they <u>absorb</u> spills. You have probably heard your teacher say that he hopes you are <u>absorbing</u> everything he says.

- **acquire**—*v.* to get. An organism is born with certain traits (like big feet) and <u>acquires</u> certain traits (like knowledge and strength).

- **adapt**—*v.* to change in response to new circumstances. When we got our new science teacher, Mr. Beak, we had to <u>adapt</u> to his weird way of calling on students. He never says our names, he just looks right at the person he wants to answer. So you always have to keep looking at him! Very annoying.

- **adhere**—*v.* to stick to. Scotch Tape <u>adheres</u> to paper quite well. It does not <u>adhere</u> well to running water.

- **anatomy**—*n.* the structure of an animal or plant. Mr. Beak is teaching us <u>anatomy</u> next week. Apparently, some animal dissecting will be involved.

- **asteroid**—*n.* a big rock orbiting the sun, kind of like a mini-planet. Most <u>asteroids</u> are in between the planets Mars and Jupiter. In sci-fi movies, space ships are always getting caught up in <u>asteroid</u> belts. Just remember, they are called "belts" because they are "wrapping around" the sun.

- **atmosphere**—*n.* the layer of gases surrounding the Earth or another planet. The Earth's <u>atmosphere</u> is mostly oxygen and nitrogen.

- **atom**—*n.* the smallest unit of an element that has all the properties of that element. Everything in the world is made up of <u>atoms</u>. The <u>atom</u> bomb gets its power from the splitting of <u>atoms</u>—that's how much energy is stored up in this tiny little particle. It's kind of scary when you think about it.

- **axis**—*n.* the center around which something rotates. <u>Axis</u> is usually used when talking about a planet (like the Earth) rotating on its <u>axis</u>.

- **bacteria**—*n.* one-celled organisms. They are all around us, but you can't see them. My mom buys anti-<u>bacterial</u> soap because she thinks my sister and I are getting too many colds. She thinks it's because of all the <u>bacteria</u> on our hands.

- **biosphere**—*n.* the part of the Earth and its atmosphere where living things exist.

- **carbohydrate**—*n.* a compound composed of carbon, hydrogen,

DOUBLE MEANING
atmosphere—n.
the atmosphere
is like the mood
in a story—it's
a writer's
tool (English
language arts).

and oxygen. In foods we eat, most of the <u>carbohydrates</u> are found in sugar and starch. The night before a baseball game I load up on <u>carbohydrates</u> by eating spaghetti for dinner and two bananas for dessert. For some reason, I never sleep very well.

carnivore—*n.* meat-eater. The most ferocious <u>carnivore</u> known to mice is the house cat.

catalyst—*n.* in science, a substance that speeds up a chemical reaction. Fire is a <u>catalyst</u> for turning water into evaporated water.

celestial—*adj.* related to the stars and the universe. Planets and asteroids and suns and stuff are all called "<u>celestial</u> bodies."

cell—*n.* the smallest, most basic part of a plant or animal. A <u>cell</u> is filled with protoplasm, has a nucleus near its center, and has a membrane that keeps it all together.

centrifugal force—*n.* moving away from the center. When you swing a bucket of water around in a circle real fast, and the water doesn't fall out, that's <u>centrifugal force</u>!

chain reaction—*n.* a series of events in which one thing leads to another, which leads to another. I saw a <u>chain reaction</u> accident on the highway once when a semi jackknifed, and all of the cars behind it ran into each other.

chemical energy—*n.* energy stored in chemical compounds. <u>Chemical energy</u> is usually released in a chemical reaction when <u>chemical energy</u> changes into heat, light, or electricity.

chlorophyl—*n.* the green pigments in plants where photosynthesis takes place.

chloroplast—*n.* the part of a plant cell that contains the chlorophyll.

chromosome—*n.* the part of the cell that carries an organism's DNA (which determines its hereditary characteristics).

circulatory system—*n.* the organs that move blood around the body, including the heart, veins, arteries, and capillaries. Just think of the pipes and plumbing that circulate water in your house. They are your house's <u>circulatory system</u>.

classify—*v.* to group organisms into categories according to similar characteristics. I would <u>classify</u> Mr. Beak as weird, along with Ms. Jank and Mr. Sleever. Mrs. Fooy and Ms. Dabs I <u>classify</u> as cool.

collision—*n.* the slamming of one thing into another. When there

DOUBLE MEANING
catalyst—n.
someone who makes things happen. Usually used in social studies when talking about a movement or revolution. The feminist movement's leader, Gloria Steinem, was a catalyst for change for women in the 1960s and 1970s.

Antonym
centripetal force—n.
moving toward a center. It's what keeps the planets orbiting around the sun.

59

is a <u>collision</u> between an opponent's bat and my best pitch, that is not good.

combustible—*adj.* flammable. My science teacher tells us when a material we are working on is <u>combustible</u>. When we are working with <u>combustible</u> materials, all Bunsen burners are turned off!

component—*n.* a part of a system or machine. The <u>components</u> of my stereo are the receiver, the CD player, and the five-speaker surround sound system.

compress—*v.* to squeeze. When <u>compressed</u> enough, a soccer ball finally goes boom. That's what I learned when my mom backed the car over my ball last week.

condensation point—*n.* the temperature at which gas condenses into a liquid. Clouds formed over the soccer field when the air temperature reached the <u>condensation point</u>.

Think of a train conductor getting you from one point to the next.

conductor—*n.* a material that takes an electric current from one point to another. Copper wire is a good <u>conductor</u>. So are you, so stay away from electricity!

conservation—*n.* the protection of natural resources. <u>Conservation</u> is important if we are to keep the few natural wonders this country has left, like the Grand Canyon and Yellowstone National Park.

contaminate—*v.* to make impure. Lots of things we do every day <u>contaminate</u> the environment. Driving a car <u>contaminates</u> the environment with carbon monoxide and other gases. Eating fast food <u>contaminates</u> the environment with all of the packaging it comes in, not to mention the pollution from the factories that make the packaging. It's almost like if you don't live in an underground house fueled by solar panels and windmills, you are <u>contaminating</u> the environment! About all we can do is try to reduce the amount of <u>contaminants</u> we produce, but we can never eliminate them.

continental drift—*n.* the theory that the continents are always drifting—they are not fixed. The continents drift only an inch or so each year, but over millions and billions of years, those inches turn into thousands of miles.

contour map—*n.* a map that shows elevations and surface configurations with contour lines. <u>Contour maps</u> are great for seeing what a region's topography looks like, but they are terrible for finding your way from one place to another.

convection—*n.* the process of heat moving across something that is unequally heated. When you are taking a bath and you give it a shot of really hot water, and that shot of hot makes the rest of the water a little bit warmer, that's <u>convection</u>.

crustal plate—*n.* one of the giant pieces of land that make up the Earth's crust.

current—*n.* 1) the flow of electricity. 2) the continuous movement of water.

cyclical—*adj.* happening in cycles. In chemistry, the word <u>cyclical</u>

has to do with chemical compounds that have atoms arranged in a closed chain. In real life, lots of things are <u>cyclical</u>. The changing of seasons is the most obvious example.

cytoplasm—*n.* the protoplasm outside the cell's nucleus.

decay—*v.* to rot; to break down. When you die, unless you have yourself cryogenically frozen or you are cremated, your body will <u>decay</u>. I plan on going the cryogenically frozen route, like in the original *Austin Powers* movie. Groovy baby, yeah!

decompose—*v.* to rot; to break down. See *decay* above. <u>Decomposition</u> is a chemical reaction.

dehydrate—*v.* to remove the water from. <u>Dehydrated</u> food like beef jerky has had the water taken out—that's why it's all shriveled. A few games ago I got <u>dehydrated</u> and started feeling dizzy because I didn't drink enough water and it was 98 degrees out.

density—*n.* the mass of an object divided by its volume. Metal is more <u>dense</u> than wood. Hot fudge is more <u>dense</u> than whipped cream.

deplete—*v.* to use up. One of the main problems today is the gradual <u>depletion</u> of Earth's resources.

deposit—*v.* to leave. Rivers and streams <u>deposit</u> sediment as they wear away the earth they run through.

deteriorate—*v.* to get worse. When you hear someone say "His health is <u>deteriorating</u>," that means it is getting worse. When you hear someone say "That house is <u>deteriorating</u>," that means it is falling apart because no one is keeping it up.

digestive system—*n.* the parts of your body that work together to break down food so it can be converted into energy. Your <u>digestive system</u> is made up of the alimentary canal, which is basically every part of your body the food touches, from your mouth all the way down to . . . well, you know.

dissolve—*v.* to mix with a liquid. Kool Aid <u>dissolves</u> in water to make a tasty, refreshing drink!

distill—*v.* to purify by evaporation and then condensation. <u>Distilled</u> water has had all of the impurities boiled out. What they do is boil the water and then capture the steam—that steam doesn't have any of the impurities that were in the water. They then drop the temperature on the steam and—ta da!—<u>distilled</u> water.

dominant trait—*n.* when paired with a recessive trait, this is the trait that "wins"—the <u>dominant trait</u> beats the recessive trait. So if the <u>dominant trait</u> in a species of butterfly is big wings and the recessive trait is little wings, a butterfly that has one gene for each will have big wings.

dormant—*adj.* sleeping; inactive. Lots of animals, insects, and plants go <u>dormant</u> over the winter, sleeping until spring. When a baseball team's bats go <u>dormant</u>, that means no one is getting any hits, and the team is doomed.

drag—*n.* the resistance of air molecules to a body moving through them. So the body (like an airplane, for instance) has to have more thrust force

Whenever you see a word with "plasm" in it, you know it has something to do with cells.

I have found that when I don't read regularly, my vocabulary starts to deteriorate.

Science

than the air molecules have <u>drag</u> force if the body is to move forward.

dynamic—*adj*. related to energy and motion. The Los Angeles Lakers have been a more <u>dynamic</u> team since Kobe Bryant started sharing the ball with his teammates. There is more motion in the offense, and they run fast breaks better.

eclipse—*v*. to block the light. When the moon <u>eclipses</u> the sun, it's always a big deal. It's all over the news and people make special <u>eclipse</u> viewers out of paper and cardboard boxes. It's bigger than Groundhog Day! (As you have probably heard a million times, never look at an <u>eclipse</u>. It could blind you.)

ecosystem—*n*. the combination of organisms and the place they live. Our apartment is an <u>ecosystem</u> all by itself, with its people, plants, pets, and other little friends like spiders and mice!

electron—*n*. a tiny particle in an atom's nucleus that has a negative charge. There are the same number of protons (+) and <u>electrons</u> (–) in an atom's nucleus. Their opposite charges cancel each other out.

element—*n*. a substance that has only one kind of atom. There are 118 <u>elements</u>. My favorite is helium, because it's the <u>element</u> that makes your voice high and squeaky.

endocrine system—*n*. the body's endocrine glands, ductless organs that secrete hormones directly into the blood. The <u>endocrine system</u> includes the thyroid, pituitary, and adrenal glands, plus a bunch more I don't have room to list here. (See "The Body" exercise for all of the organs involved in your <u>endocrine system</u>.)

endothermic—*adj*. absorbing heat. Think of <u>indoors</u> for <u>endothermic</u> reactions. It's a reaction that brings heat "inside."

entropy—*n*. disorder or chaos in a system. So if the Los Angeles Lakers have three of their best players injured, they have <u>entropy</u> on the team: disorder and chaos.

environment—*n*. a person's, animal's, or plant's surroundings. My favorite <u>environment</u> is the baseball field. I feel most comfortable out there on the mound.

equilibrium—*n*. a condition in which all forces cancel each other out, resulting in balance. Remember it by thinking of the word "equal." <u>Equilibrium</u> happens when opposing forces are equal.

erosion—*n*. the process of being worn away, usually by water or wind. A huge windstorm in Cape Cod caused a lot of <u>erosion</u>—all the sand on the beaches was basically blown into the Atlantic.

eruption—*n*. the explosion of a volcano. The <u>eruption</u> of Mount Vesuvius in A.D. 79 ended up burying two entire cities in lava and ash. They have only recently started excavating the site.

evaporation—*n*. the process of a liquid turning into a gas. I left a glass of Kool Aid on my bedroom window sill and forgot about it. A few weeks later, all the liquid had <u>evaporated</u>, and all that was left was red, crusty goo. (Also see the definitions for *distill* and *condensation point*.)

Name five organisms that are part of an ecosystem at or near your home.
1.
2.
3.
4.
5.

Anto**nym**

exothermic—adj. releasing heat. Think of an EXIT sign for exothermic reactions.

Do an Internet search and find the most recent volcano eruption in the United States.

evolve—*v.* to change for the better. The theory of <u>evolution</u> is based on the idea that animals <u>evolve</u> to better take advantage of their environment. So if the environment is full of scary, spike-headed monsters, it would be good for a species to <u>evolve</u> in ways that would protect it from the monsters. (Thick skins and fast legs come to mind.)

exothermic—*adj.* releasing heat. An <u>exothermic</u> reaction happens when substances react strongly with each other. For example, if you mix two substances in a test tube and the tube gets hot, that's an <u>exothermic</u> reaction. Heat has been released. (See *endothermic* for more.)

extinct—*adj.* no longer in existence. The dodo bird is <u>extinct</u>—there aren't any of them on the planet any more. Dinosaurs are <u>extinct</u>. My mom says real gentlemen are <u>extinct</u>. (I'm not sure what that means.)

fault—*n.* a break in a rock formation. Earthquakes happen along geologic <u>faults</u>, where a rock formation is broken and two big slabs of rock are rubbing against each other.

fertilize—*v.* to make fruitful or productive. When an animal's egg is <u>fertilized</u>, its offspring begins to grow. When crops are fertilized, they usually produce more fruits or vegetables.

fissure—*n.* a crack in a rock. Earthquakes usually form along <u>fissures</u>, where the rock is rubbing against itself.

food chain—*n.* a series of organisms that eat each other.

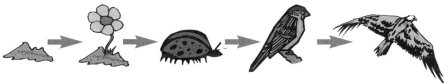

fossil fuel—*n.* fuel made from decayed organisms. Coal and oil are actually dead plants and animals that decayed and have been compressed over millions of years into <u>fossil fuels</u>. Wind is not a <u>fossil fuel</u>. Neither is solar energy. They are renewable resources. (See the definition for *renewable*.)

friction—*n.* rough rubbing. The <u>friction</u> between two rock formations is what causes earthquakes.

function—*n.* use. Every player on a baseball team has a specific <u>function</u>. As a power pitcher, my <u>function</u> is to strike batters out.

fusion—*n.* in physics, a reaction in which atoms join together. In chemistry, when two substances are melted and mixed together. Basically, <u>fusion</u> takes place when two separate things <u>combine</u> into one thing.

gene—*n.* a section of a chromosome that controls how part of an organism turns out. You have <u>genes</u> that control your eye color, your height, your looks—everything. And we are learning more and more about <u>genes</u> every day. Scientists just completed charting every <u>gene</u> —it was called the Human Genome Project.

generation—*n.* a group of organisms born around the same time; a stage in a succession. I have heard people calling our <u>generation</u>

Name three more extinct animals or species.

1. _____
2. _____
3. _____

Think of a name for your generation that is better than Generation I.

_____
_____

63

"Generation I" because we are the first to grow up with computers and the Internet.

genetics—*n*. the study of genes and heredity. The field of genetics is really booming right now. All of the stuff they are finding out about genes and how they affect our health and everything about us is really cool. Some people even think genetics will be the key to curing cancer!

glaciation—*n*. the process of being overtaken by glaciers. Right now glaciation is in retreat. Instead of glaciers covering more of the Earth, they are melting. The Ice Age was a time of incredible glaciation.

greenhouse effect—*n*. the result of too many pollutants in the atmosphere; they let the sunlight in, but they don't let the heat back out. That causes the atmosphere to act like a greenhouse—keeping the heat in. Some people think the greenhouse effect is causing all the glaciers to melt around the polar icecaps.

habitat—*n*. the normal environment where an organism lives. A water turtle's natural habitat is a pond. A hermit crab's natural habitat is the ocean. That's why, when we have them as pets, we try to re-create their habitat inside an aquarium with rocks, sand, water, and some driftwood to climb on.

hemisphere—*n*. in earth science, the northern or southern half of the Earth. The equator is what separates the Northern and Southern Hemispheres. To remember it, think hemisphere = half-a-sphere.

herbivore—*n*. an animal that eats plants. Cows are herbivores. Horses are herbivores. Vegetarians are herbivores. They all eat veggies, no meats.

heredity—*n*. the passing down of traits from parent to offspring.

hierarchy—*n*. a group organized by rank. In the hierarchy of students at school, baseball players come in somewhere above the glee club and somewhere below the soccer players.

hybrid—*n*. the offspring you get when you breed two different kinds of parents. You most often hear the word hybrid when people are talking about plants, like a corn hybrid that fends off insects or a hybrid tomato that is bigger and juicier than any other kind of tomato.

hydrosphere—*n*. the world's waters. All the oceans, seas, lakes, rivers, streams, and puddles make up the hydrosphere.

hypothesis—*n*. a proposed explanation or statement. Scientific progress is based on proving or disproving a hypothesis. If your hypothesis is "plants are mean," and you do an experiment that proves plants are mean, then your hypothesis is correct. If the experiment does not prove plants are mean, that DOES NOT mean the hypothesis is incorrect, only that your experiment didn't prove it.

igneous rock—*n*. rock that is formed from molten lava. It's not metamorphic, it's not sedimentary—it's igneous!

ignite—*v*. to light on fire. When you ignite your Bunsen burner in science class, it gives off a blue flame.

Whiz Fact

The United Nations did an environmental study that concluded that the greenhouse effect is going to raise the temperature 2–10 degrees in the next 100 years.

DOUBLE MEANING

hemisphere—n. also stands for one-half of the brain—the left and right hemispheres.

Whiz Quiz

Identify the rock's type:

basalt

_____

granite

_____

limestone

_____

marble

_____

immune—*adj.* being resistant to something. You often hear this word when people are talking about AIDS. AIDS is an acronym for Acquired Immunodeficiency Syndrome. It's a disease that attacks your <u>immune</u> system, and makes it so you can't fight off any bacteria or other bad germs.

incinerate—*v.* to burn until there is nothing left but ashes. If you flew a space shuttle toward the sun, the sun's heat would <u>incinerate</u> it.

inertia—*n.* resistance to motion. My dad has a lot of <u>inertia</u> on weekends. It's hard to get him off the couch.

interact—*v.* to be involved with something else. Science is always testing how different things <u>interact</u>. It can be chemicals that <u>interact</u> with each other in an experiment, it can be animals <u>interacting</u> with each other in a habitat, it can be how the orbits of planets <u>interact</u> with each other.

interchangeable—*adj.* switchable. Teachers are not <u>interchangeable</u>. When Mr. Beak was out for a week getting a hernia operation, we got a substitute who gave us a ton of homework every night. It was a terrible week.

ion—*n.* an atom or molecule that used to be electrically neutral, but now it is either positive or negative because it gained or lost electrons. In other words, it used to be neutral (same number of protons and electrons) but it has since gained or lost an electron, so it is a positive <u>ion</u> (lost electrons) or negative <u>ion</u> (gained electrons).

kinetic energy—*n.* energy generated by movement. When a hitter's bat connects with my fastball and sends it out of the park, that, unfortunately, is <u>kinetic energy</u>. To remember <u>kinetic</u>, think of *calisthenics*. They kind of sound the same, and they both have to do with movement.

kingdom—*n.* a division of organisms. The Bengal tiger is part of the animal <u>kingdom</u>. The daisy is a member of the plant <u>kingdom</u>.

land subsidence—*n.* the sinking of land. In some arid regions of the Southwest, tapping the water in the water table has resulted in <u>land subsidence</u>. As water is sucked out, the land actually sinks!

lift—*n.* a force working against gravity. When you <u>lift</u> your book off the table, you are exerting a greater <u>lift</u> force than gravity is exerting.

light year—*n.* the distance light travels in a vacuum in one year (9.46×10^{12} kilometers). It's important to remember that a <u>light year</u> is a measure of distance, not time.

lithosphere—*n.* the Earth's crust. All of the valleys, mountains, plains, and meadows, plus all of the bottoms of the seas, rivers, and lakes, make up the <u>lithosphere</u>.

lunar—*adj.* having to do with the moon. A <u>lunar</u> eclipse is when the Earth blocks the sun's light from the moon. The <u>lunar</u> module is a spaceship that landed on the moon.

magma—*n.* the molten rock below the Earth's surface, waiting to spew out in a volcano and then form igneous rock when it cools. I went on a vacation to Hawaii and I actually saw red, glowing <u>magma</u> where there are active volcanoes.

magnitude—*n.* in earth science, a measure of the amount of energy released by an earthquake. Earthquakes' <u>magnitudes</u> are always measured. Small earthquakes have <u>magnitudes</u> from 2–3. Medium-size earthquakes have <u>magnitudes</u> from 4–6. Large earthquakes have <u>magnitudes</u> from 7–10.

mantle—*n.* the layer of rock between the Earth's crust and its core. So, we walk all over the crust, the core is boiling molten rock, and the only thing keeping the molten rock from us crust-dwellers is the <u>mantle</u>. Thank you, <u>mantle</u>!

mass—*n.* the physical volume of a solid body.

matter—*n.* something that occupies space; stuff.

meiosis—*n.* cell division in sexually reproducing organisms that produces a cell with half the required number of chromosomes that will then link up with the other half of the chromosomes from the other sex partner. Humans have 46 chromosomes—23 from each parent. <u>Meiosis</u> is what produces one of those 23-chromosome sex cells (called gametes).

membrane—*n.* as in cell <u>membrane</u>, the outer layer of the cell. The <u>membrane</u> keeps all the stuff inside the cell from floating out AND it keeps out the stuff the cell doesn't need.

metabolism—*n.* the chemical and physical processes that take place in cells; the changes that take place in a body. You have probably heard people say "I have a high <u>metabolism</u>—I eat anything I want all day and I don't gain a pound." Someone with a high <u>metabolism</u> has a body that is working really fast and efficiently to burn up all the food it gets.

Related Word

metamorphosis—n. the change from one thing to another.

metamorphic rock—*n.* rock that was changed from one kind of rock to another by pressure or temperature. It's not sedimentary, it's not igneous—it's <u>metamorphic</u>!

mineral—*n.* a natural substance with a definite chemical and crystalline composition. A diamond is a <u>mineral</u>. So are gold and silver.

mitochondrion—*n.* the part of the cell that converts food into energy the body can use. It's at the last stage of digestion, working to turn that burger and fries into energy for your body.

mitosis—*n.* the division of a cell into two identical cells; the process of cell division.

mixture—*n.* something made up of a lot of different stuff.

molecule—*n.* the smallest unit of a compound or an element. A <u>molecule</u> of water has two hydrogen atoms and one oxygen atom—H_2O.

molten—*adj.* melted or liquefied by intense heat. The lava that comes out of volcanoes is <u>molten</u> rock.

mutation—*n.* a change in the genes of an organism from one generation to the next. The theory of evolution states that a <u>mutation</u> that helps an organism survive better than others will be passed down from generation to generation, because that organism and its offspring will have a better chance of living and having kids. That's why giraffes have long necks. They lived in a place where the food was up high, so the ones with the genetic <u>mutation</u> that gave them longer necks did better and had more kids than the ones with shorter necks who couldn't get to the food and died.

natural selection—*n.* the theory that organisms best suited for their environment survive and have offspring, and those who are not die and do not have offspring. Also known as "survival of the fittest." Kind of harsh, I know. But it is the way things work in nature. (See *mutation* for more on this.)

neutron—*n.* a particle that's in the nucleus of all atoms (except hydrogen). A <u>neutron</u> has the same mass as a proton, but no electrical charge (it is neutral). So the nuclei of atoms have protons, electrons, and <u>neutrons</u> (except hydrogen, which has only electrons).

nuclear energy—*n.* the energy released by a nuclear reaction. <u>Nuclear energy</u> makes up a big part of this country's energy production, but not nearly as much as energy produced by burning oil, coal, and natural gas. The thing is, <u>nuclear energy</u> plants can be much more dangerous than other energy sources. If something goes wrong and radiation escapes from a nuclear power plant, people can get sick and die.

nucleus—*n.* 1) in a cell, the center of a cell containing the genes. The <u>nucleus</u> of a cell contains the parts that control the cell, like the <u>nucleus</u> of a baseball team is made up of the players who control whether a team wins or loses. 2) In an atom, the center of the atom containing protons, electrons, and neutrons.

offspring—*n.* the "children" of an organism. Sexually produced <u>offspring</u> inherit half of their genes from each parent.

omnivore—*n.* an organism that eats all kinds of food, including plants and animals. Humans are <u>omnivores</u>. So are dogs.

orbit—*n.* the path of one celestial body around another. Planets travel in different <u>orbits</u> around the sun.

organelle—*n.* a specialized part of a living cell that functions like an organ.

organic—*adj.* having to do with living organisms. When you see food labeled "organic" in the grocery store, that means it was grown

Related Word

magma—n. red-hot rock beneath the Earth's crust.

Whiz Quiz

Name a genetic mutation that helped this species survive:
Giraffe
Human
Elephant
Cheetah

Whiz Fact

Two famous dangerous nuclear accidents:

Three-Mile Island, 1979 Pennsylvania, USA

Chernobyl, 1986 Chernobyl, Ukraine

Related Word

herbivore and carnivore (See the definitions in this chapter.)

with all <u>organic</u> materials—no chemicals or man-made substances were used.

organism—*n.* a living plant, animal, bacterium, protist, or fungus. I have used the word <u>organism</u> in tons of these science definitions. It's obviously because lots of science is concerned with the study of <u>organisms</u> and all of the things that affect <u>organisms</u>.

oxidation—*n.* a reaction in which the atoms in an element lose electrons. The most common example of <u>oxidation</u> is the formation of rust. Metal atoms <u>oxidize</u>—they lose electrons—and rust forms.

ozone layer—*n.* a layer of our atmosphere that protects us from harmful sun rays. Pollution is causing holes in the <u>ozone layer</u>, which means those bad sun rays are making it all the way down to the Earth, where they can cause skin cancer. My mom always makes me wear sunscreen when I play baseball because she's worried about the holes in the <u>ozone layer</u>.

particle—*n.* a small part; a speck.

periodic table—*n.* the chart that lists all of the elements and their atomic numbers.

5	6	7	8
B	C	N	O
13	14	15	16
Al	Si	P	S
31	32	33	34
Ga	Ge	As	Se

photosynthesis—*n.* the process that plants use to turn sunlight into energy. If people could perform <u>photosynthesis</u>, we wouldn't need to eat so much! We could just sit in the sun and get all the energy we need. Instead we have to cover ourselves in sunscreen and stay in the shade. Lucky plants.

physiology—*n.* all of the vital parts and processes of an organism.

potential energy—*n.* the energy something has that is derived from its position or structure, not its motion.

precipitation—*n.* rain, snow, sleet, and hail. The weatherman said the odds of <u>precipitation</u> tomorrow are 50 percent. But he's never right.

predator—*n.* an animal that hunts another. A shark is a fierce <u>predator</u>, hunting other fish continuously, never sleeping, always hungry.

propulsion—*n.* driving force. The engines on a plane provide its <u>propulsion</u>.

protein—*n.* a compound in all living things that helps organisms grow and repair themselves. Good sources of <u>protein</u> are beef and beans and eggs—which all happen to be in my favorite omelet!

proton—*n.* a positively charged particle in an atom. (See definitions of *electron* and *neutron*.)

protoplasm—*n.* a jellylike substance that forms all the living matter in plants and animals. That's right, the basis for all living things is a jiggly mass of jelly. Kind of gross when you think about it, so I try not to.

Related Word
predatory—adj.
like a hunter.

prototype—*n.* an original version of something that later versions are based on. I saw a bunch of electric car prototypes at the auto show last year. I liked the three-wheeled one best.

protozoa—*n.* primitive, single-celled organisms. Protozoa might be what the earliest forms of life on Earth were like.

radiation—*n.* the emission of waves or particles. Nuclear radiation is waves and particles given off by radioactive material. It can be really dangerous and even lethal.

recessive trait—*n.* when paired with a dominant trait, it is the trait that "loses."

renewable—*adj.* able to be used again. Most often used in the term "renewable resources" to describe sources of energy that can be used again and again. Two examples are wind and sunlight—they are forms of energy that you basically can use over and over, and they never get used up.

reproduction—*n.* the process by which living things produce offspring. Most animals and plants use sexual reproduction, where the offspring gets half its chromosomes from each parent. In asexual reproduction, the offspring gets all its genetic material from one parent. The formation of spores is a good example of asexual reproduction.

respiratory system—*n.* the group of organs that keep you breathing. If you think of it in terms of your house, things that circulate air—like fans and air conditioners—are your house's respiratory system. (See the "The Body" exercise for all of the organs involved in your respiratory system.)

revolve—*v.* to move in a circular motion around a center. The Earth revolves around the sun. The San Francisco Giants revolve around their best player, Barry Bonds.

satellite—*n.* a man-made object shot into space that orbits the Earth or another planet. Most satellites these days are used for communication, but there are also science satellites and military satellites.

scientific method—*n.* the process of observing something, forming a hypothesis for how it works, doing experiments to test that hypothesis, and then drawing conclusions from your results. *Example*: After watching bears at the zoo, you form the hypothesis that bears are dumb as rocks and you do an experiment to test their intelligence. Maybe you ask them their names. When they don't the answer, you conclude your hypothesis is correct—they don't know their names, they must be dumb as rocks. (You can see why the scientific method isn't perfect!)

sedimentary rock—*n.* rock that is formed near the Earth's surface by the accumulation of sediment. It's not metamorphic, it's not igneous—it's sedimentary!

selective breeding—*n.* the process of choosing which plants or animals to breed with each other. You do this when you are looking to promote a particular trait. So if you are breeding poodles and you

The Incredible Hulk was created when scientist Bruce Banner was accidentally exposed to radiation.

The first satellite was launched by the Russians in 1957. It was called Sputnik.

want poodles with extra long toes, you <u>selectively breed</u> the long-toed poodles. (You give the short-toed poodles away to friends.)

shear—*n.* force working in an opposite but parallel sliding motion to a body's planes.

solar—*adj.* having to do with the sun. The <u>solar</u> system is the system of planets revolving around the sun. <u>Solar</u> flares are eruptions that spew from the sun and mess up our television reception. <u>Solar</u>caine stops sunburn pain when someone you love is hurting.

soluble—*adj.* dissolvable. Sugar is <u>soluble</u> in water. So is Kool Aid.

solvent—*n.* a liquid that dissolves another substance. Water is a <u>solvent</u> for many substances, including sugar, salt, and Kool Aid.

stagnant—*adj.* motionless; not flowing. When water is <u>stagnant</u>, it becomes a prime breeding ground for mosquitoes. When my soccer team's offense gets <u>stagnant</u>, we start booting the ball downfield and just going for broke.

stimulus—*n.* something that causes a response. An organism is always responding to both internal and external <u>stimuli</u>. For example, a toad responds to <u>external stimuli</u> like predators and temperature and <u>internal stimuli</u> like hunger and the urge to reproduce.

suspend—*v.* to float; to remain undissolved. When I sprinkle fish food flakes in my sister's fish tank, they remain <u>suspended</u> in the water for a few minutes before they sink to the bottom.

sustainable—*adj.* able to be maintained over a period of time. One of the ways to fight world hunger is to find <u>sustainable</u> crops that starving countries can grow themselves. There is a Chinese proverb: "Give a man a fish and he will eat for a day. Teach a man to fish and he will eat for the rest of his life." That's the idea behind teaching people in these countries to grow <u>sustainable</u> crops.

synthesis—*n.* the combination of two or more things to make a brand new thing. I think the *Star Wars* movies are the perfect <u>synthesis</u> of special effects and a great story. Combining those two things has made a brand new thing—the best movie series ever.

tectonic plate—*n.* one of the huge plates that make up the continents and the floors of the oceans. They shift a little all of the time. The friction where the <u>tectonic plates</u> meet causes scary stuff to happen, including earthquakes, mountains, and tidal waves.

tension—*n.* a force that stretches or elongates something. By applying <u>tension</u> to my T-shirt, I was able to stretch its tiny head-hole over my big fat head.

thrust—*n.* a force that moves a body forward. The <u>thrust</u> of the engines propelled the airplane forward.

tissue—*n.* a bunch of cells that, together, are considered one thing. The human body is made up of all kinds of <u>tissues</u>, including muscle <u>tissue</u>, organ <u>tissue</u>, and scar <u>tissue</u>.

topography—*n.* the physical aspects of a place or region. The word is often used in the phrase "<u>topographical</u> map," which is a map that

Remember, <u>sol</u>uble things can be dis<u>sol</u>ved.

What kinds of sustainable crops do they produce in your part of the state?

shows a region's physical landscape instead of roads and landmarks.

torsion—*n.* a force that twists something. The <u>torsion</u> I applied to the stuck lid was finally enough to twist it off of the peanut butter jar.

toxic—*adj.* harmful; dangerous. Scientists deal with <u>toxic</u> materials all of the time. Sometimes we even work with them in science class ourselves. Stuff like mercury and dry ice is pretty cool, but they can be very <u>toxic</u>, so be careful.

trait—*n.* a characteristic; a feature. I share a lot of physical <u>traits</u> with my dad—we both have brown eyes, high foreheads, and winning smiles.

transform—*v.* to change from one thing into another. Coal is <u>transformed</u> into diamonds under intense pressure after millions of years.

transmitter—*n.* an instrument that sends signals, usually waves of some sort (light, sound, radio).

vacuole—*n.* a cavity in the protoplasm of a cell.

vacuum—*n.* a space where there is no matter. Lots of science experiments have to be done in a <u>vacuum</u> to work. For example, in a <u>vacuum</u>, an eyelash and a deep dish pizza fall at the same rate, because there is no matter—air—to make the eyelash fall more slowly.

vapor—*n.* stuff that looks like mist, fumes, or smoke. Steam is the <u>vapor</u> form of water.

velocity—*n.* speed. The highest <u>velocity</u> I have ever thrown my fastball is 72 miles per hour.

vital—*adj.* necessary to life. Surgeons closely monitor the <u>vital</u> signs of their patients, like blood pressure and heart rate.

watt—*n.* the fleshy orange fold of skin under a turkey's neck. Wait—that's a wattle. A <u>watt</u> is a unit of electricity. If you want to save electricity, make sure all the light bulbs in your house are 40-<u>watt</u> or 60-<u>watt</u> bulbs.

weight—*n.* the measure of how heavy something is. This is determined by how much gravity is acting on a body. A light thing (eyelash) is subject to low gravitational pull. A heavy thing (large deluxe deep dish pizza) is subject to high gravitational pull.

Nature is full of transformations. Name three:

1. _____
2. _____
3. _____

To remember vital, think of your favorite TV hospital drama. When they ask for "vital signs," they are asking for the signs of life.

WhizWords

biosphere
conservation
ecosystem
environment
equilibrium
fossil fuel
greenhouse effect
habitat
hydrosphere
lithosphere
organism
sustainable

Related Word

renewable—adj.
Fossil fuels are
not renewable.
You use them
once, and they
are history.

Science

The Environment

Have you ever heard of Woody Guthrie? He was a folk singer who wrote hundreds of songs about America. He would travel the country hitchhiking and riding on freight trains, getting to know the people he met along the way. He ended up writing classics like "This Land Is Your Land," "Pastures of Plenty," and "Do-Re-Mi." (No, not the song about "a female deer" and "a drop of golden sun." A different "Do-Re-Mi.")

Guthrie was also a big environmentalist. He was really alarmed by all of the factories he saw going up around the country. He saw America as an expanse of forests and plains and deserts and lakes and rivers. And he saw it changing into an expanse of roads and cities and houses and, well, people.

My dad loves Woody Guthrie. He is always humming "This Land Is Your Land" and putting in his own words. So when he has to cut the grass he likes to sing, "This land is your land, this land is my land, I've got to cut the grass, that'll keep me smilin'." It can get annoying, but it gave me a great idea for how to remember environment words.

WRITE A FOLK SONG EXERCISE

What I want you to do is use each of these "Environment" words in a verse of "This Land Is Your Land." You want to squish the word and the definition into the verse. It may not win you any Grammys, but if you spend some time on it and fit all twelve words into twelve verses, you'll have a little hummable song about the environment. And you can hum it during a test if you need to remember the words!

I'll get you started with a verse about the WhizWord off to the side—*renewable*.

♫ This land is your land,
This land is my land,
Use *renewable* fuels and
The air won't stink like trash cans. ♫

Like I said—it's not going to win any Grammys. If you have another song you want to use instead of "This Land Is Your Land," by all means, go ahead. If you've never even heard "This Land Is Your Land," ask your music teacher to hum a few bars, or go on the Internet to www.geocities.com/Nashville/3448/thisl1.html to hear a snippet.

WhizWords

**anatomy
circulatory system
digestive system
endocrine system
respiratory system**

Science

The Body

By the end of middle school you should have a pretty good idea of what the different parts of the human **anatomy** do. The four main systems of the body aren't that hard to understand, but there are a lot of organs in each one, so it's good to be able to organize the organs by the systems they are in.

Just remember: the **circulatory system** has to do with circulating the blood. The **digestive system** has to do with organs that help you digest your food. The **respiratory system** does your breathing for you (to remember the word, think about being put on a respirator—a machine that breathes for you). And the **endocrine system**, well, it helps get the bad stuff out of your blood. Crime is bad—so think about the **endocrine system** getting the bad stuff out of your blood. Close enough!

LABELING YOUR INNARDS EXERCISE
I have listed the major organs in each system. Your challenge is to label them in this Britney Spears body outline. Check the answer key when you are done.

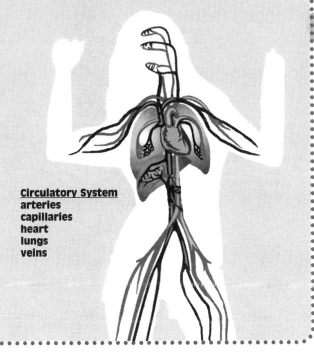

Circulatory System
arteries
capillaries
heart
lungs
veins

Science

Digestive System →
anus
esophagus
large intestine
mouth
small intestine
stomach

Respiratory System
diaphragm
lungs
nose
pharynx (throat)
ribcage
trachea

The Body

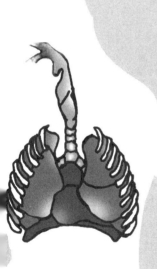

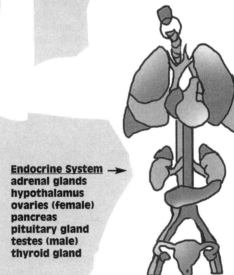

Endocrine System →
adrenal glands
hypothalamus
ovaries (female)
pancreas
pituitary gland
testes (male)
thyroid gland

WhizWords

asteroid
atmosphere
axis
eclipse
light year
lunar
orbit
ozone layer
satellite
solar

Related Word

celestial—adj.
**Asteroids and
satellites are
both** celestial
**bodies, because
they are both
part of the
universe.**

Science

Planets and Space

Sometimes I just lie on my back in my backyard at night and look up at the sky and imagine what the astronauts on the International Space Station must think when they look out the window. Have you ever seen the movie *Apollo 13* or spent any time on NASA's website? The pictures of space from the windows of spacecraft are just incredible.

And now it looks like normal citizens are going to be able to go into space, just like the astronauts. In 2001, an American businessman named Dennis Tito became the first space tourist when he paid $20 million to join a Russian space crew on a trip to the International Space Station. So someday, you may get to travel in space, whether you're an astronaut or not.

DRAWING THE UNIVERSE

For this exercise you get to draw and label the universe, from the perspective of an astronaut on the old Mir. I have provided the Earth, its moon, and the sun. You can draw and/or label the rest of the "Planets and Space" words above on this page, or draw everything yourself (which I recommend). For example:

LABEL OR DRAW
● distance to sun in *light years*
● a partial *eclipse*
● the moon's *orbit*
● a *satellite*

Science

Genetics

My friend Gene has curly red hair and freckles just like his father and all of his brothers. That's how I remember that a **gene** is the part of the cell that decides which characteristics will be passed from one **generation** to the next.

But sometimes **genetics** don't work out quite so logically. For instance, my sister Esther is really tall: 5'9". Both of my parents are short. So am I. So what happened to Esther? There must have been a **recessive** "tall" **gene** that both of my parents carried that, against the odds, made it into my sister. The same goes for her eye color. My parents both have brown eyes. I have brown eyes. My sister has blue eyes. So what happened to Esther? Again, a **recessive trait** in both my parents ended up being expressed in my freaky sister. Here's how that happens:

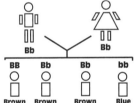

As you can see, the odds are great that my parents would have children with brown eyes, because that is the **dominant** gene for eye color. All you need is one brown eyes gene to have brown eyes. Esther just got lucky and received a **recessive** "blue eyes" **gene** from each of my parents.

MOVIE AND TV STAR RECESSIVE TRAITS

Pick out two movie stars. I am going to pick Cher and Billy Crystal. Now, pick a trait. I am going to pick foot size and make big feet dominant and little feet recessive. Draw a chart like the one I drew above, giving each either two dominant genes (FF), two recessives (ff), or one of each (Ff). See how their children would turn out. Here is my Billy + Cher drawing.

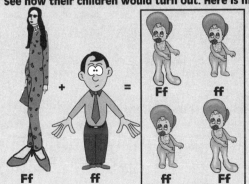

I don't even want to think about what the rest of their bodies would look like.

Exercises

WhizWords

compress
continental drift
contour map
crustal plate
deposit
erosion
fault
fissure
friction
glaciation
igneous rock
mantle
metamorphic rock
mineral
molten
sedimentary rock
tectonic plate
topography

Science

Topography

My family likes going camping. We have been all over the place in the past few years: the Sierra Nevadas, the Smoky Mountains, the Colorado Rockies. Last year, we went hiking in the Berkshires out in Massachusetts. All of the Berkshire mountains are very, very old. They're tiny little hills compared to the newer, higher, steeper versions out West. In fact, their highest peak, Mt. Greylock (3,491 ft.), isn't even a foothill compared to the country's highest peak, Mt. McKinley (20,320 ft.), in Alaska.

Of course that wasn't always the case. At one point, Greylock was much taller than it is now. See, mountains are usually formed where two **crustal plates** meet and cause a lot of **friction**. The plates are forced up into the sky. Then, over millions of years, **erosion** wears the tall, new mountains into short, old ones. So the **topography** of a region often depends on how long ago the **compression** of plates took place, the size of the mountains formed, and what kind of **deposits** were left behind as the mountains **eroded**.

MOUNTAIN TAKEOVER

Like I said, the Berkshires are basically in a state of constant *erosion* at this point (geologically speaking). There aren't a lot of new mountains being formed by the violent meeting of two *crustal plates*.

But what if that wasn't the case? What if, instead, Massachusetts was a hotbed of plate activity? What if it was like California, but instead of plates moving across and away from one another like they are out there, they were moving toward each other, and after each big earthquake (an earthquake is caused when plates rub against each other) there was a new mountain standing?

I want you to use the "Topography" words above to write a short science-fiction story where you imagine a relatively flat place being beset with huge mountains the size of Mt. McKinley. You can get started on the page to the right. Here's the first paragraph of my story, just to give you an idea. I've written mine as a news item, but you can write yours any way you want. Heck, write a poem for all I care! Just use as many of the "Topography" words as you can.

New Mountain Disrupts Traffic Outside Boston
By Grady Goode

Commuters were tied up in traffic for miles Wednesday morning when yet another mountain burst through the Earth's *mantle* just outside Boston. Local officials were ready for the new peak, however, as increased *friction* between two *crustal plates* had been measured in the area over the previous days. "The new mountain broke through a bunch of old *sedimentary rock*" said Mayor McCheese as he surveyed the area. "I'm just glad it didn't cause any deep *fissures* in the surrounding area."

Mountain Takeover

_____

_____

_____

_____

_____

_____

_____

_____

_____

_____

_____

_____

_____

_____

_____

_____

_____

_____

Chapter 5
Test Instructions

Use your pencil when you have reading passages on tests. Underline the topic sentence of each paragraph and circle proper names. It will help you pace yourself and it will also help you when you refer back to the passage for information.

approximately—*adj.* close to; almost the same as. Sometimes tests ask you to approximate—that means you are supposed to use the information they give you to make an estimate. *Example:* Based on the data, approximately of how many bites it will take to eat the entire pizza?

clue—*n.* something that helps answer a question or solve a problem. Clues are your friends. If a test gives you clues, spend time reading them. *Example:* Which graph fits all of these clues?

compare and contrast—*v.* show the similarities and the differences. Tests love for you to compare and contrast things because it's a great way for them to figure out if you understand what you are reading and writing.

compute—*v.* to perform a math operation. *Example:* Compute 4/5 + 3/4.

conclude—*v.* to form an opinion based on information. *Example:* What can the reader conclude from this article? (In other words, what did the reader (you) get from reading this passage?)

convince—*v.* to persuade. As in "information to convince the reader . . . ." Some tests ask you if an author provided enough examples to convince you of something. So if I wanted to convince you the Arizona Diamondbacks are going to win the World Series this year, I'd have to provide reasons to persuade you.

corresponds—*v.* matches; agrees with. Sometimes you are asked to pick the answer that corresponds to the data in the question. That just means it matches. So a test may have a statement like:

The *Star Wars* trilogy became the highest grossing movie series ever, earning more than $1 billion.

And then it says:

Pick the statement that corresponds to the data given in the statement:

    A) The *Star Wars* trilogy lost money.

    B) The *Star Wars* trilogy won three Oscars.

    C) The *Star Wars* trilogy made a lot of money.

    D) The *Star Wars* trilogy was directed by Blythe Danner

describe—*v.* to explain. Some questions provide several descriptions for you to choose from. *Example:* Which word best <u>describes</u> Germany's economy? Others ask you to do all of the <u>describing</u> yourself. *Example:* <u>Describe</u>, in your own words, how Jerry fared at the comedy club.

detail—*n.* fact or evidence. Reading comprehension questions often ask you to provide <u>details</u> from a passage to support your answer. They are just making sure you understand what you just read. *Example:* Use <u>details</u> from the newspaper article to support your answer.

estimate—*n.* approximation. *Example:* What is the best <u>estimate</u> of the angle formed by first, second, and third base?

evidence—*n.* proof. When tests ask for <u>evidence</u>, they want you to prove that you know the answer and aren't just making a wild guess. *Example:* Provide <u>evidence</u> for your answer using details from the story.

explain—*v.* to describe; to offer reasons for. Like asking for evidence, asking you to <u>explain</u> yourself is another way tests find out if you really know what you are talking about. *Example:* <u>Explain</u> how you came to your answer.

expression—*n.* a way of saying something, usually with an equation. As in "Which <u>expression</u> could be used . . ." or "Which <u>expression</u> represents . . . ." So you are trying to match the <u>expression</u> to the passage. A passage may say:

Tim bought five eggs, dropped three, and then purchased five more. Which <u>expression</u> represents Tim's egg-buying experience?

    A) $5 + 3 + 5$
    B) $5 - 3 - 5$
    C) $5 - 3 + 5$
    D) $g + h + i$ (The answer is C.)

fact—*n.* something that actually happened or actually exists. As in "Which of these is a <u>fact</u> in this passage?" And when there is a question about <u>fact</u>, there is often a question about opinions, too. (See *opinion* for more.)

identify—*v.* pick out; choose. You can think of <u>identifying</u> questions as a police line-up. The question lines up a bunch of

81

ugly guys, and you have to <u>identify</u> the one who fits the right description. *Example:* <u>Identify</u> the adjectives and adverbs in the following paragraph.

label—*v.* to mark with a name or sign; to identify. Some questions want you to identify things with a <u>label</u>. Think of the <u>labels</u> on cans of soup. How would you tell tomato from mushroom without a fancy <u>label</u>? *Example:* <u>Label</u> the shapes with their appropriate names.

main idea—*n.* the most important thought. Tests sometimes ask you to identify the <u>main idea</u> of a reading passage. You get a <u>main idea</u> by reading a passage carefully. Sometimes the title of a reading passage offers a clue about the <u>main idea</u>. Sometimes it's better to decide the passage's <u>main idea</u> *before* you read the answer choices. You will usually find your <u>main idea</u> among the answer choices. But if you read the answer choices first, it can get confusing, because usually all the answer choices are ideas from the reading passage, but they aren't all the <u>main idea</u>.

most likely—probably. This means the answer is what is probably going to happen. At least there is a better chance it will happen than the other answers. The answer to a <u>most likely</u> question usually isn't spelled out in the reading passage. You have to guess what is <u>most likely</u> to happen based on the information in the passage. *Example:* Which <u>most likely</u> was served first, dinner or dessert?

opinion—*n.* something someone believes or thinks, whether it is true or not. As in "Which is an <u>opinion</u> in this passage?" Being able to tell the difference between facts and <u>opinions</u> is important for the reading sections of many tests. (See the definition of *fact* for more on this.)

pattern—*n.* plan; diagram; model. <u>Pattern</u> questions ask you to figure out an answer by giving you a group of numbers or symbols that repeat at some point. *Example:* What is the sixth number in this <u>pattern</u>?

probably—*adv.* most likely. Tests use phrases such as "<u>probably</u> felt . . ." or "<u>probably</u> believes . . ." or "<u>probably</u> thought . . . ." It just means that the passage doesn't actually state what a character or writer believes, but from reading it, you should be able to tell anyway.

purpose—*n.* goal; reason. Questions that ask for a <u>purpose</u> usually want you to figure out the larger goal involved in a piece of writing. *Example:* What is the writer's <u>purpose</u> for titling his essay "A Call to Arms"?

reasonable—*adj.* logical; showing good judgment. <u>Reasonable</u> is like "best." *Examples*: "Which is a <u>reasonable</u> total cost . . ." and "What is a <u>reasonable</u> prediction . . ." and "What is a <u>reasonable</u> conclusion . . ." and "What is a <u>reasonable</u> length . . . ." Who is the most <u>reasonable</u> person you know? The most <u>reasonable</u> person I can think of is the newsman Tom Brokaw. You know who I'm talking about—he reads the nightly news for one of the networks. He

Whiz Tip

Think of the main idea as the "main tent" at a circus. That's where the main show with the elephants and the trapeze artists is. The other parts of the circus are in smaller tents. They are all part of the circus, but the main tent is the main idea. So when you look at the answer choices, think "Is this the elephant in the main tent, or the bearded lady in a smaller tent?"

Whiz Tip

Trust your instincts on these probably questions. If you think a writer probably meant to say the Earth is flat, and that is an answer choice, you are probably right.

seems very <u>reasonable</u>—like I can trust him. Whenever I get a question asking "What is a <u>reasonable</u> . . . whatever," I think—which answer would Mr. <u>Reasonable</u>, Tom Brokaw, choose? You can do the same thing. Just pick out the most <u>reasonable</u> person you know and try to choose the answer you think he would choose.

represent—*v.* to stand for; to take the place of. *Example:* Let *x* <u>represent</u> the length of the pool.

statement—*n.* explanation. Sometimes you have to choose from among a group of <u>statements</u>, and sometimes you have to write your own. *Example:* Write a <u>statement</u> that explains which beaker will fill up first.

suggest—*v.* lead you to believe. It just means the information doesn't come right out and say something, it just hints at it. It's kind of like a "probably" question—you have to read the passage carefully and trust your understanding of it. *Example:* What does the information in the passage <u>suggest</u> about the town of Trent?

summarize—*v.* to explain briefly. *Example:* <u>Summarize</u> the events that led up to the Battle of the Bulge.

support—*v.* to provide evidence for. This means you can't just state your opinion or give an answer. Not only do you have to give the right answer, you have to show how you got it. *Example:* Use details from the article to <u>support</u> your answer.

WhizWords

describe
detail
evidence
explain
main idea
purpose
support

Test Instructions
Reading Carefully

Related Word

conclude—v.
**to form an opinion based on information.
Tests are always asking you what you can** conclude **from a reading passage.**

As you know by now, being able to read things and understand what you read is very important when it comes to doing well on tests. The way tests often figure out how well you understand things is by using these "Reading Carefully" words. So it helps if you get used to answering questions that use these words, no matter what kind of reading it is.

My favorite things to read are, in order, the online *USA Today* sports page, *Sports Illustrated*, and the Harry Potter series. So as long as J. K. Rowling keeps pumping out books; baseball, basketball, and football players don't go on strike; and *USA Today* keeps going strong, I am going to be reading for the rest of my life. You probably have some favorite reading materials, too. That's what we are going to use in this next exercise.

READING WHAT YOU LIKE
Open your favorite book, magazine, or newspaper, or go to your favorite website. Pick a passage or article that's about one to three pages long. If you use a website, print out the article. Read it carefully, using your pencil to circle important names and underline important sentences. Take your time, really "get into" the writing. When you are done reading, write three sentences using at least three of the "Reading Carefully" words:

Describe author's *purpose* in this article.
What *details* from the passage *support* this?
The *main idea* of this passage is:

Do this with at least five different kinds of writing, rotating the "Reading Carefully" words as you go. If you like doing it, do it a lot. It takes, like, five extra minutes, and you'll end up remembering a ton more stuff about things you actually like.

WhizWords

estimate
probably
reasonable
suggest

Test Instructions
Probably

Not everything in life is absolutely, positively 100 percent obviously true. Come to think of it, almost nothing is. That means you have to get used to recognizing degrees of possibility.

For example, the Los Angeles Lakers are **probably** going to be really good for a long time because they have the best one-two punch in basketball: Kobe Bryant and Shaquille O'Neal. And it's **reasonable** to **suggest** that Britney Spears is going to be popular for a long time because she's so . . . talented.

What's my point? My point is that even if you don't know something is absolutely, positively 100 percent obviously true, you can still know a whole bunch of things are **probably** true. And on tests, one of the keys to doing well is being able to figure out what is **reasonable**, and what is not.

If you are having trouble on tests figuring out what is **probably** true, a good way to get some perspective on things is to think "What would Mr. Reasonable do?" And everyone knows who the most **reasonable** people on the planet are. Newscasters!

Related Word

approximate—v. to come close to; to estimate. Math tests often ask you to approximate something, which means using the information provided to get an answer in a general range.

ASK MR. REASONABLE

If you don't watch the nightly news already, take half an hour out of your busy schedule for a few nights and watch the Big Three: CBS (Dan Rather), NBC (Tom Brokaw), and ABC (Peter Jennings). Pick the newscaster who strikes you as the most *reasonable* of the bunch—the guy who would *probably* pick the right answer. Mine is Tom Brokaw. He seems like he would make a good, *reasonable* guess.

Now get a pencil and paper. Write your guy's name on the top of a piece of paper. Now sit down with a parent or friend and watch the news! Have your news buddy write down four questions about stories from the nightly news, using the four "Probably" words. For example:

Is it *reasonable* to *suggest* that Iraqi President Saddam Hussein will make nice with President George W. Bush?

Before you answer, think "How would Tom Brokaw answer?" Do this every night for a week, and you'll probably get the hang of the "Probably" words and questions.

Hint: One way to be sure you've come up with the right answer to a question using a "Probably" word is to write a response that includes the word "because," *because* this will require you to go back to the reading passage to find information to prove your point. If you can't find evidence to back up your answer, you're *probably* wrong.

Chapter 6
All-Purpose Words

WhizQuiz

List the three classmates you collaborate with the most:

_____

_____

inconvenient—adj. causing a lot of trouble.

decrease—adj. to take away from; to lessen.

exterior—adj. outside

advantage—*n.* favorable position. You will be at an <u>advantage</u> if you know all of the words in this book. You will be at a <u>disadvantage</u> if you leave this book on the bus.

collaborate—*v.* to work together. You learn best when you <u>collaborate</u> in the classroom. My science teacher has us <u>collaborate</u> on projects, but I've been having trouble getting anyone to work with me since I accidentally lit my lab partner's Skittles on fire with a Bunsen burner.

consistent—*adj.* steady; always the same. The best way to do well on tests is to be <u>consistent</u> with your studying. Cramming for tests may work once in a while, but in the end you won't remember as much.

contradiction—*n.* something that disagrees with something else. You have probably heard the phrase "a <u>contradiction</u> in terms." That's when two words in a row <u>contradict</u> each other, like: "an angry clown." Clowns aren't usually angry, at least not in public. Tests also often ask you to find <u>contradictions</u> in stories and passages. That is where two things do not agree with each other.

contribute—*v.* to give. It is important to <u>contribute</u> to your community. I do so by volunteering at the food pantry one day a month.

convenient—*adj.* easy; handy. This book is incredibly <u>convenient</u> to keep around. It's small, and it has all the words you need to know. Just put it in your bookbag and keep it there. Whenever you have a question about a word, this book will be <u>conveniently</u> in your bag and you can look it up.

increase—*v.* to grow; to add to. Your test scores will <u>increase</u> if you know all the words in this book.

interior—*adj.* inside. Test sometimes ask you to measure <u>interior</u> and <u>exterior</u> angles. This just means the angle on the inside or the outside of the figure.

logical—*adj.* reasonable; making sense. <u>Logical</u> is kind of the opposite of *emotional*. When you get emotional on tests, you can really mess up. Try to stay <u>logical</u> as much as you can, going from one question to the next without getting too worked up.

maximum—*adj.* the very most. The <u>maximum</u> score you can get on most tests is 100%. The <u>minimum</u> is 0%.

outcome—*n.* result. Tests often ask for you to pick the right answer from a group of <u>outcomes</u>. That just means you need to pick the right result. *Example:* Which <u>outcome</u> is most likely?

precise—*adj.* exact; accurate. Tests kind of go back and forth from asking you to be <u>precise</u> with your answers to asking you to estimate (make a reasonable guess). So make sure you pay attention to <u>precisely</u> what the text question asks for.

predict—*v.* to guess in advance. Some test questions ask you to <u>predict</u> what will happen in an experiment or in a story. That means you are supposed to look at the facts and make a logical guess as to what will happen. (See definitions of *logical* in this section and *conclusion* in English Language Arts.)

relevant—*adj.* related to the matter at hand. Sometimes on tests, you are asked to use only <u>relevant</u> information—that means information that matters (as opposed to stuff that does not matter). For example, if you are taking a test on making cheese, milk is <u>relevant</u>, because it's an ingredient in cheese, while information on fingernails is not <u>relevant</u> (it is <u>irrelevant</u>).

similar—*adj.* alike. Nomar Garciaparra and Derek Jeter are quite <u>similar</u>. They are both excellent fielding shortstops who hit for power and average.

systematic—*adj.* acting according to a plan or system. <u>Systematic</u> is a lot like *strategic*—they both are used a lot when talking about a powerful person, like a general or dictator, who has a master plan and a *strategy* or a <u>system</u> to carry it out.

tangible—*adj.* touchable; real. This book is <u>tangible</u>—it is real and you can touch it. The word is used a lot in the phrase "<u>tangible</u> benefits," which means good things that actually happen. For example, my friend Lamonte realized the <u>tangible</u> benefits from all his time in the kitchen when he won first prize in the cake baking contest.

**minimum—adj.
the very least.**

**Try to predict your
grade on a
test before you
take it, then
see how close
you are to your
prediction.**

**irrelevant—adj.
not pertaining
to the matter
at hand.**

**intangible—adj.
not touchable.**

WhizWords

All of 'em.

All-Purpose Words
Celebrity Hot Tub

You can also do this with flash cards—write the word on one side, and the question using the word's definition on the other.

Did you ever want to be one of those reporters on *Entertainment Tonight* or *Extra* or *Access Hollywood* who just spends all her time running around, interviewing celebrities at parties? Or better yet, a VJ on MTV who just hangs out and chats with bands and singers who come by the show's studios? Well, I have.

My idea is that I'd have the celebrities over to my house and interview them sitting in my parents' hot tub. We'd relax in our swim suits, sip lemonade, and talk about whatever they wanted to talk about. I'm actually thinking about doing this for my public access cable station or doing a webcast. I just haven't figured out how to arrange the microphones without all of us getting electrocuted.

CELEBRITY HOT TUB

For this exercise you are going to need a pad and pencil. Write down "Celebrity Hot Tub" at the top of a page. Now, go to one of the chapters and write down ten words that you are having trouble with. Just read through the words and definitions from one chapter and pick out ten words where you are still a little shaky. Here are ten I picked from Social Studies:

communism	pivotal
dominate	provoke
ethics	revenue
import	subversive
intervene	Whig

Now form a question that you would ask a celebrity who joined you for Celebrity Hot Tub. Use the definition as part of your question. For example, this is a question that I would ask supermodel/actress James King.

Q: Ms. King, what is the most *pivotal* role in your acting career? By that, I mean, which role do you think will help you become the next Barbra Streisand?

After you have written questions using ten words from one chapter, go ahead and write questions with words from the other chapters, too. Keep these all in one place so you can go back and review them (or ask them, should you ever find James King sharing your hot tub).

All-Purpose Words
Word of the Day

You know those daily calendars that look like a block of Post-it Notes? You peel off a page every day and learn something new—every day. My favorite one is the *Far Side* cartoon-a-day calendar. I even have a bunch of my favorite *Far Side* calendar pages taped to the inside of my locker. My favorite one is "The Night of the Crash Test Dummies"—it has all these crash test dummies attacking some poor guy in his car.

Anyway, the cool thing about that calendar and others like it is that you get to see something new every day. And that's the best way to learn vocabulary words, by using them every day.

Related Word

consecutive—adj. occurring in order, one right after the other. For this exercise, you are going to be learning words consecutively, one right after the other.

VOCABULARY CALENDAR
Until I can convince my book's publisher to make a WordWhiz word-a-day calendar, you are going to have to make one for yourself! This exercise will take an afternoon, so wait until you have a few hours to kill—maybe when it's raining out or you are home sick from school—to get started.

You can make this calendar one of two ways:

> With a brick of Post-it Notes
> With some other "something-a-day" calendar

If you use Post-its, first go through them and make them into a calendar, writing down the days and months left in this year. (Use a wall calendar as a guide.)

If you use another calendar, find one that has a lot of empty space where you can write down a word and its definition.

Now, there are another 600 words in this book. You need to choose the 365 words (or however many days are left on your calendar) that you need to learn the most. Now write the word and its definition on your calendar.

When you are done, put your calendar somewhere where you will see it the first thing in the morning: by your bed, on the sink in the bathroom—wherever. Read the word-of-the day aloud, repeat it and its definition three times, then put it in your pocket. Try to use that word as much as you can on its day.

Word Whiz

Answer Pages

Here are my answers to the Whiz Quizzes and Exercises.
To find out how you did on quizzes and exercises that ask you
to write essays, create calendars, and otherwise use
your creativity, run your answer past an adult who can decide whether or not
you have used the vocabulary words correctly.

English Language Arts

Whiz Quizzes
page 8
Use an adjective or adverb to
describe each of these words:

I go to a *small* school.

My mom had a *fabulous* shopping
experience last week—she got four
pairs of shoes for the price of one.

Difficult tests make me
concentrate even harder.

My soccer team has *bright*
green uniforms.

I play a lot of *physical* sports, like
soccer and football.

The pizza at lunch today was
unbelievably chewy. It was like
eating pizza-flavored gum.

Use an analogy to a staircase to
describe how your grades have been
going recently:

I'm trying to improve my grades, but it's
easier to run down a flight of stairs than it
is to climb them.

page 11
List three euphemisms you or
members of your family use:

If I don't get *Tomb Raider*
I'm going to lose it.

Grandpa Goode is a few cards
short of a full deck.

If the Red Sox lose again
I'm going to be ill.

page 12
Identify the part of speech
of the following words:

blonde—adj., n.
threaten—v.
fake—adj., n., v.
mambo—n., v.

Note: As you probably ca[n]
tell by now, many words
have meanings that have
multiple parts of speech.

page 13
Write the following sentences
using metaphors:

Pam is <u>greased lightning</u>.

James is <u>two French fries short of a
Happy Meal.</u>

Fabio <u>vacuums up</u> ice cream
like there is no tomorrow.

page 15
Briefly summarize the last book you read:

The Old Man and the Sea
An old man hadn't caught any fish in
quite some time, then he caught the
biggest fish anyone had ever seen and
had to bring it in to shore all by himself.

Social Studies

Whiz Quizzes
page 29
List three things you once
thought were futile:

1. Reaching a height of five feet.

2. Achieving the high score on
Arctic Thunder.

3. Mastering the remote control for
our new TV.

Who was the first president
to be impeached?

President Andrew Johnson

page 32
Go to www.house.gov and find a piece of
legislation Congress is working on now.

The House passed the
Sensenbrenner/Jackson-Lee anti-discrimi-
nation legislation by a vote of 420-0.

page 34
Name your favorite team's
main opposition:

The New York Yankees

page 36
List three regulations at your school:

1. No chewing gum in class.
2. For boys, no T-shirts: all
   shirts must have collars.
3. For girls, no skirts: only
   dresses and slacks.

page 39
Name a limitation you have
had to transcend in your life:

I was really impatient a few years
ago and got upset over unimportant
things. I have worked hard to
be more patient and mellow.

Exercises
page 41
Government

Country	Year	Government
England	1714	Monarchy
Texas	1836	Republic
United States	1897	Democracy
Germany	1935	Fascism
Jordan	1953	Monarchy
Cambodia	1976	Despotism
England	1979	Democracy

Answer Pages

Math

Whiz Quizzes
page 47
Pick the next number in
these number patterns:

3, 6, 9, 12, <u>15</u>
–3, –1, 1, 3, <u>5</u>
3/4, 1 1/2, 2 1/4, <u>3</u>

page 49
Circle the integers.
1/2
.6
(6)
(–6)
(–2)
(0)
3.2
6.9
3/4
(17)
(–12)
(243)

page 53
Solve the following problems
with the variables x=2 and y=3:

$2x = 2(2) = 4$
$4y = 4(3) = 12$
$x - y = 2 - 3 = -1$
$2y + 7x = 2(3) + 7(2) = 6 + 14 = 20$
$-2x - 4y = -2(2) - 4(3) = -4 - 12 = -16$

Exercises
Number Types
page 56
$.79
positive number, rational number

.327
positive number, rational number

2 1/2
positive number, rational number

4
integer, positive number,
rational number, whole number

-12
integer, negative number, rational number,
whole number

6π
irrational number, positive number

Number Relationships
page 57

	Mean	Median	Mode
English	85.71	92	92
Math	85.43	82	78
Science	94.43	94	94
Social Studies	83.86	84	84
O'Neill	.291	.285	.256
Ramirez	.313	.309	none
Rodriguez	.300	.305	none
Garciaparra	.321	.357	none
Gwynn	.336	.329	.317

Science

Whiz Quizzes

page 62
Name five organisms that are part of an ecosystem at or near your home.

1. flies
2. Bob the cat
3. mice
4. tomato plants
5. ants

Do an Internet search and find the most recent volcano eruption in the United States.

The Kilauea volcano on Hawaii continues to spew stuff on a daily basis.

page 63
Name three more extinct animals or species.

1. Dodo bird
2. Tasmanian tiger wolf
3. Sea cow

Think of a name for your generation that is better than Generation I.

Generation Perfect

page 64
Identify the rock's type:

Basalt—igneous
Granite—igneous
Limestone—sedimentary
Marble—metamorphic

page 67
Name a genetic mutation that has helped this species survive:

Giraffe—long neck
Human—opposable thumbs
Elephant—big tusks
Cheetah— extreme speed

page 70
What kinds of sustainable crops are produced in your part of the state?

In Boston, where I live, none. But further west, they grow some corn.

page 71
Nature is full of transformations. Name three:

1. Caterpillars transform into butterflies.
2. Ice transforms into water (and vice versa).
3. Seeds transform into flowers.

Answer Pages

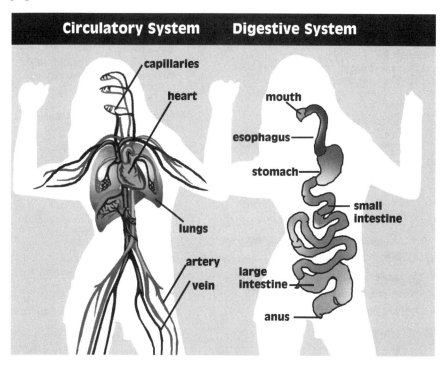

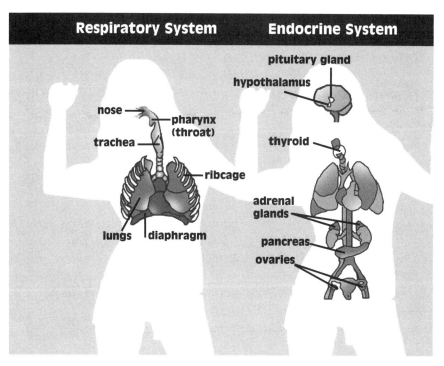

Test Instructions

Whiz Quizzes

page 81

Provide one piece of evidence supporting each
of the following statements:

1. Christina Aguilera is really weird.
Just look at her hair!

2. Plants need water to live.
When I forgot to water Mom's favorite fern, it died.

3. Mountain Dew without the carbonation tastes awful.
I made three of my friends taste a day-old. half-full can.
None of them are friendly with me now.

All-Purpose Words

Whiz Quizzes

page 86

List the three classmates you
collaborate with most:

Frank
Judy
Mookie (until the stale Mountain Dew incident)

Also Available

Crusade in the Classroom:
How George W. Bush's Education Reforms
Will Affect Your Children, Our Schools